learn to STUDYTHEBIBLE

Forty different step-by-step methods to help you discover, apply, and enjoy God's Word.

Andy Deane

Learn to Study the Bible
Forty different step-by-step methods to help you
discover, apply, and enjoy God's Word

Published by Xulon Press
www.xulonpress.com

First printing, 2009

Cover design by Chris Rypkema

Editing by Noreen Hay

ISBN 978-1-60791-576-8

Printed in the United States of America

For more information, or to order additional copies of this book, visit the author's website: www.LearnToStudyTheBible.com or call (888) 271-2551.

Special thanks to my wife Shannon for all of your support during this writing project. Your handwritten examples make these methods understandable and attainable. You are such a blessing to me and you're a godly helpmate.

ENDORSEMENTS

Wow, Andy has shattered the cold stone ceiling of Bible study! No longer will the Bible remain mysterious, or reserved for theologians. Many Bible study methods morph into boring laborious monotony, but not this one. *Learn to Study the Bible* makes knowing the Bible adventurous, deeply personal, thought provoking, and just plain fun. No matter where you open this book you will discover great new methods of digging into the treasure of God's Word. Whether it is the chapter on Daily Devotions, the Rethink and Restate Method, or the Verse-by-Verse charting, you will find the next page is as helpful and enjoyable as the last. Anyone wishing to cultivate the same passion for God's Word that has transformed the author will love this book.

Pastor Lloyd Pulley
Senior Pastor of Calvary Chapel Old Bridge, in New Jersey

Andy has put together an amazing resource. We will definitely be using it as part of our training for all our leaders and School of Ministry students, as well as for our one-on-one discipleship sessions, and small group Bible studies.

Pastor Bob Caldwell
Senior Pastor of Calvary Chapel Boise, in Idaho

Bible study is overlooked and under-appreciated by many Christians. This book takes it from a scholar's level and helps people understand that ANYONE can study the Bible! It is very applicable, and since it presents so many different methods, there is sure to be one (or a few) that will fit every reader.

Pastor Kevin Miller
Jr. High Youth Pastor of Calvary Chapel Albuquerque, in New Mexico

TABLE OF CONTENTS

The Foundations of Bible Study
Core components of every Bible study

Basic Bible Study Methods
Simple ways for everyone to study God's Word

Major Bible Study Methods
Time-tested approaches for those who want to go deeper

Creative Bible Study Methods
Interesting methods that add variety to Bible study

Studying Specific Passages
Diverse techniques for studying certain biblical topics

Study Methods for Younger Students
Basic Bible study methods suitable for teenage students

Wrapping It All Up
Instruction for continued growth as a student of the Bible

Visit **www.LearnToStudyTheBible.com** for exculsive bonus web content.

FOREWORD

Nothing could be worse than turning the living Bible into a boring and confusing tome. Yet, that is exactly what happens to so many, simply because they haven't been given the essential tools needed to unlock the rich character of God's Word for themselves.

As "people of the Book," we Christians have received a privilege that truly is above all else. And yet, so often I hear believers expressing frustration in their attempts to study and understand God's Word. Either they tell me they don't know how to get started, or they get bogged down in boring and monotonous study routines, or they don't know the basics of being able to observe, interpret, and apply biblical principles in their own lives.

That is why I am so excited about this book. Andy Deane has provided the church with an exceptional answer to this problem, by giving the reader all the tools needed to grow in their understanding and love for God and His Word. In this one resource, Andy has done an amazingly thorough job of compiling a wide variety of Bible study methods and describing them in a way that is useful, concise, and practical. Frankly, I am surprised that no one has done this before.

I believe *Learn to Study the Bible,* is a valuable resource for every Christian who wants to dig deeper into God's Word, and also for anyone who has the opportunity to teach the Bible to others. It is a book that can be opened randomly to almost any page, and on it you will find a new and exciting way to encounter the Word of God. I look forward to hearing how God uses it in the lives of His children.

Pastor Dave Rolph

Calvary Chapel Pacific Hills
Aliso Viejo, California

Dave Rolph has been involved in ministry at Calvary Chapel for over thirty years. Dave was an assistant pastor at Calvary Chapel of Costa Mesa for 25 years, and is currently serving as senior pastor of Calvary Chapel Pacific Hills in Aliso Viejo, California. He is heard daily on his radio program, The Balanced Word, and was the general editor of The Word For Today Bible, by Pastor Chuck Smith.

The Foundations of Bible Study

Core Components of Every Bible Study

Every house needs to be constructed on a solid foundation, if it is going to stand strong during adverse conditions. So too, Christians who build their lives upon the solid rock of God's Word, will have the strength needed to weather all of life's storms. The following chapters contain useful helps and basic information that are the essential building blocks for Christians who desire to study God's Word. Spend some time reviewing these chapters before digging into the various methods.

The Joy of Bible Study

I rejoice at Your word as one who finds great treasure.

— Psalm 119:162

Imagine this hypothetical situation: You are asked to sift several tons of sand from one pile to another, by spooning it through a hand-held strainer. Without a doubt you would consider that kind of a task to be futile and boring. However, what if you were told that while doing this you were guaranteed to find a gold nugget every hour, and as you continued sifting through the pile you would begin finding them every minute. In addition, whatever treasure you found would be yours to keep. No longer would the task seem futile or boring. The pile of sand would take on a whole new meaning to you because of the value that was hidden within.

The same analogy can be made of Bible study. With very little effort, great riches are ours to discover and keep, as we carefully sift through the Word of God each day. With access to such great spiritual treasure, we can relate to the words the psalmist wrote in Psalm 119:162.

Gold, Diamonds, and Emeralds

Exactly what kind of treasure can we expect to find in the Bible? I've heard Psalm 19:7-10 rephrased by someone this way: "The revelation of God is whole and pulls our lives together. The signposts of God are clear and point out the right road. The life-maps of God are right, showing the way to joy. The directions of God are plain and easy on the eyes. God's reputation is twenty-four-carat gold, with a lifetime guarantee. The decisions of God are accurate down to the nth degree. God's Word is better than a diamond, better than a diamond set between emeralds. You'll like it better than strawberries in spring, better than red, ripe strawberries."

That is my prayer for everyone who reads this book. May you become skilled at discovering God's great treasure, and be excited by the spiritual riches that are yours to keep, as you learn to study the Bible.

Eight Benefits of Studying the Word

1.	It assures us of salvation 1 John 5:13	5.	It guides our decisions Psalm 119:105
2.	It cleanses us from sin John 15:3 / John 17:17	6.	It helps us in prayer John 15:7
3.	It gives peace John 16:33	7.	It strengthens 1 John 2:14
4.	It brings joy John 15:11	8.	It leads to success Joshua 1:8

The Bible Answers Life's Biggest Questions

In addition to discovering the richness of our Creator, studying the Bible also helps us to learn more about ourselves, and the world in which we live. Answers to all of life's biggest questions are found in God's Word.

Questions such as:

- Who am I?
- Why am I here?
- Where did I come from?

- Where am I going?
- What should I do with my life?
- What's my relationship to God?

The Bible answers all of these questions and many more. From cover to cover, the Bible is God's revelation to us.

Who Should Study the Bible?

Every Christian should study the Bible. We all need God's wisdom no matter what season of life we are in. This little poem, written by a Baptist church in Indiana, answers the question well:

The young—to learn how to live; the old—to know how to die

The ignorant—for wisdom; the learned—for humility

The rich—for compassion; the poor—for comfort

The dreamer—for enchantment; the practical—for counsel

The weak—for strength; the strong—for direction

The haughty—for warning; the humble—for exaltation

The troubled—for peace; the sinner—for salvation

The doubting—for assurance; all Christians—for guidance

Why I Wrote This Book

This project came about after, what I thought was going to be a fairly simple task of teaching a group of junior high students a few basic inductive Bible study principles that would help them dig into the Word on a daily basis. The class wasn't forced upon them; they wanted to learn how to study the Bible for themselves. So, I agreed to share some of what I have learned about studying the Scriptures with them. I even threw in some clever (or at least I thought so) illustrations and examples that teenage minds could relate to, in an attempt to make the class fun and memorable. But to my surprise, after forty minutes they were actually worse off then when we began; all I had to show for my effort was a room full of frustrated and confused teenagers. The collective look of bewilderment on their faces was one of the scariest moments I've ever experienced as a youth pastor. I had accomplished the exact opposite of what I had set out to do: instead of getting them excited about studying the Bible, they left feeling as though it was totally out of their reach.

What a disaster! I quickly realized that the biggest mistakes I made were 1) trying to teach them a method of Bible study that was too complicated for them to grasp, and 2) presenting it to them as if it was the only way to study Scripture. I was determined to right this wrong, but first I needed to do a little research. So, I began to look for the perfect Bible study method—one that would open their young minds to the richness of God's Word.

A personal quest began to grow out of my utter failure. Every day I searched for new study methods. I read over thirty books (many out of print) and visited countless websites looking for the best Bible study methods. None of the ones I found were perfect, but many of them had interesting points of view and seemed like they would be fun to try. So I did. That is when I began to realize that I was onto something more than I anticipated at the start. My search resulted in not one, but numerous inspiring and challenging Bible study methods suitable for any Christian, young or old, who desires to draw nearer to the Lord through studying His Word.

In the end, I had compiled a list of forty different step-by-step Bible study methods. I tested each of them myself, modifying some in order to make them a little more efficient and to the point. As I was doing this, a desire to share my discoveries with others began to intensify in my heart. I wished that everyone could read the books and visit the websites for themselves, but I knew that wasn't realistic. So I did the next best thing. I decided to bring it all together in this one book, *Learn to Study the Bible.*

No other resource provides the large variety of Bible study methods, handwritten examples, and study aids that are available in this one book. The hundreds of hours spent researching and experimenting with these forty methods will enable you to find one or more that will fit your goals and begin enhancing your understanding of God's Word, today. Whether you are a teenager or a mature Bible student, a Sunday school teacher or a pastor, a stay-at-home mom or a busy executive, you will find in the pages of this book, a number of Bible study methods that will add excitement and enjoyment to your study of God's Word. In addition, you will have resources at your fingertips that will help you to train and encourage others who want to learn how to dig into the Scriptures for themselves.

Why Use a Method to Study the Bible?

It has been rightly said, if we fail to plan, we plan to fail. This is true when it comes to Bible study too. If you have a desire to study the Bible but don't have a plan, you will fail. But the good news is: You now have many plans to choose from! When it comes to methods for studying the Bible, variety is the spice of life. Unfortunately, Christians don't always realize this. Instead, many leave the study of Scripture to their pastor or Bible study teacher simply because they never learned how to study the Bible, or the Bible study method that they were taught was too complicated for them to work into their daily lives.

Each of the forty methods compiled in this book have been tested and enjoyed in my own personal study time and shared with many of my students and friends. They all offer unique perspectives that will inspire every Christian to dig deeper into God's Word, no matter how long he or she has been a believer. Although diverse in style, one element common to them all is that they cause you to think through the Scriptures and get the most from your reading of God's Word. I recommend that you try each of these methods. They will help you:

- Stay fresh in your approach to God and His Word.
- Draw out great spiritual truths from the Scripture passage that you may have missed otherwise.
- Avoid the dryness that can sometimes creep into routines.

In addition, I want to make this one last point. As nice as it is to dine at a fine restaurant, nothing beats sitting down to a delicious home cooked meal. The same can be said of feasting on the Word. In the body of Christ we have been gifted with many wonderful Bible teachers who serve up hearty meals that help us come to a better understanding of certain passages. However, the real meat and potatoes of growing in truth comes when we roll up our own sleeves and learn how to prepare those meals for ourselves. Learning to study the Bible is as easy—and diverse—as learning how to cook your favorite foods. Don't let anything rob you of experiencing the best God has for you, personally, in His Word today.

The forty methods we will be looking at in this book are sure to satisfy every appetite. Yes, it will take some work and a little planning, but in the end, I guarantee it will be well worth the effort. One verse of Scripture well chewed, digested, and assimilated into your life will strengthen and satisfy your hungry soul more than anything else this world has to offer. So get your Bible and a notebook, and let's dig in!

chapter

01

Tips for Profitable Bible Study

The entrance of Your words gives light

— Psalm 119:130

M ost believers understand the value and necessity of Bible study. However, knowing the importance of studying God's Word and actually doing it are not the same thing. Some Christians struggle when it comes to studying the Scriptures simply because they have never been taught. They listen to others who teach the Bible and walk away thinking, "How did they ever get all that from that one passage?" A lack of instruction in the basics of Bible study—not an ignorance of the need for it—is the reason many feel unable to understand God's Word for themselves.

The Transition from Reading to Studying Is Writing

One reason Christians don't benefit more from their time in God's Word is because they fail to recognize one important distinction: Reading the Bible is not the same as studying the Bible. While I recommend that every Christian be committed to a daily Bible reading schedule; it is equally important to set aside time each week for a more in-depth Bible study. The difference between reading and studying comes down to one factor: writing. Regardless of the method of Bible study that works best for you, the first rule of thumb in studying Scripture is to have a pen and a notepad on hand.

Bible study is not something that can be done in our heads. Every study method involves some form of writing. Whether it is answering questions, rewriting a verse, or making a list; writing helps us to slow down, reflect upon, and work through the passage we are reading. Unless we jot down our thoughts, questions, applications, and observations, we will quickly forget what we have read. But when we pause long enough to put our thoughts on paper, our scrambled first impressions will work themselves out of our heads through our fingertips and into our hearts and lives. By disciplining ourselves in this way, we will spend more time considering what God is saying to us in His Word and learning how it applies to our lives. That is exciting!

> **REMEMBER:** *Developing a habit of writing down what God is revealing to you as you read His Word is the first and most important step in studying the Bible, and it is something you can begin doing today. By dedicating a notebook or journal to be used during your study time, or even writing your thoughts in the margin of your Bible, you will begin to transition from reading to studying.*

How Much Effort Will It Take?

Studying the Bible is a spiritual discipline that requires both time and effort. In the physical world, everyone knows that it takes more energy to digest meat than milk. The same can also be said of the spiritual world. Assimilating the "meat" of Scripture requires more effort than sipping on the "milk" of the Word. Sometimes we make the mistake of thinking that because it is a spiritual pursuit it should not be labor intensive. However, with little perspiration you will find little inspiration. So, yes, Bible study is work, but the riches that you will discover as you dig into the Bible will be well worth the time and energy you devote.

A.B. Simpson wrote, "God has hidden every precious thing in such a way that it is a reward to the diligent, a prize to the earnest, but a disappointment to the slothful soul. All nature is arrayed against the lounger and the idler. The nut is hidden in its thorny case; the pearl is buried beneath the ocean waves; the gold is imprisoned in the rocky bosom of the mountains; the gem is found only after you crush the rock which encloses it; the very soil gives its harvest as a reward to the laboring farmer. So truth and God must be earnestly sought."

Don't Let Your Enemy Discourage and Distract You

I'm convinced one of Satan's most successful schemes against God's people is in blinding us to the importance and relevance of spending time studying the Scriptures. God's Word is invaluable. It is a far greater treasure than anything this world has to offer yet many treat it as though it has no worth. Instead of investing time studying the Bible, it is left unopened and gathering dust. Whether it is because of busyness, complacency, or just a lack of awareness, believers miss out on the benefit of growing in their relationship with the Lord when they do not cherish and abide in His Word.

Satan's primary objective is to prevent Christians from appropriating all that is rightfully ours as God's children. He wants us to live spiritually bankrupt and destitute lives. One of the ways in which he goes about accomplishing that is by keeping us from studying God's Word. It is simple really: If we don't know who we are or who our God is, then we will miss out on what He wants to do in and through our lives. God has given us a surpassing treasure according to the riches of His glory—we have every spiritual blessing in Christ. But unless we are grounded in biblical truth, we are destined to be ineffective for the gospel. However, when we make time to study the Bible, our lives are enriched and established upon the sure foundation of His Word.

When we understand this, we will begin to rightly esteem its value and importance in our daily lives. We will also view the time we spend in God's Word as the most vital part of our days and guard that time from being disturbed by the constant stream of distractions that make up our modern lives. Ringing cell phones and never-ending emails are always clamoring for our immediate attention, but as we discipline ourselves to set time aside to study God's Word we will realize that intrusions such as these will be better handled after we have spent time with the Lord.

Prerequisites for Good Bible Study

The way you approach your time of Bible study will determine how fruitful it will be. For a productive time in God's Word please consider these three essential ideas before starting:

1. <u>NEW BIRTH:</u> Only born again believers can truly enjoy Bible study. Spiritual thoughts will not make sense to the natural man because the spiritual side of him has yet to be born. Paul tells us in 1 Corinthians 2:14, "the natural man does not receive the things of

the Spirit of God, for they are foolishness to him; nor can he know them, because they are spiritually discerned."

2. <u>HOLINESS:</u> God has set us apart for His purposes. If we insist on indulging in sin, the sincere milk of the Word won't settle well in our stomachs and we will probably end up with indigestion or no appetite at all. What we do when we are away from the Bible greatly affects how clearly we will hear God speaking to us when we are reading His Word. If you have a great Bible study method, but a hard heart, your time in God's Word won't benefit you that much.

3. <u>PRAYER:</u> Always begin your study time in prayer asking the Lord to reveal His character and nature through the passage being read. Time spent in prayer before studying the Bible is non-negotiable. The unaided human mind is incapable of grasping the Bible's eternal message. One benefit of studying the Bible, as compared to studying any other subject, is that we can talk with the Author through prayer.

Look for Jesus Everywhere

One of the main reasons why we study the Bible is to get to know the Author better. That is why setting a goal for our Bible study that focuses solely on gaining knowledge and facts, misses the point. Look for clues in the text that reveal God's attributes and meditate upon what you are learning about Him in His Word. When we study the Bible with the under-standing that it is God's love letter to us, it will help us to get to know Him more intimately. The Scriptures lead us directly into God's heart, so missing Him in all our studying would be a failure to grasp the most important lesson. By seeking to know the Lord better through our study of His Word we will begin to cherish that time and long for more of it each day because it is the place where we get to meet with Jesus. Best of all, when the day finally comes and we stand before Him face-to-face, we will not be doing it as strangers.

Christ is the key to understanding the Scriptures (John 5:39-40). One exciting discovery you make as you study the whole Bible is finding that Jesus Christ is the centerpiece of each of the Bible's sixty-six books. He is in everything: the law, the prophets, and the psalms (Luke 24:25-27). So when we see a priest in Scripture, it reminds us that Jesus is our High Priest. When we see a king or a shepherd, it is a type of Jesus, our Chief Shepherd. When we see a sacrifice, we remember Jesus is the Lamb of God who takes away the sins of the world. Everything in the Old Testament foreshadows, and points to, Jesus. Everything in the New Testament reflects back on the life, death, burial, and resurrection of Jesus. Search diligently for Jesus in every passage—He is there!

The Main Goals of Bible Study

In James 1:21-25, we learn that one of the most important goals of spending time in God's Word is that we would be changed by it. James compares the Word of God to a mirror that helps us to observe ourselves in light of God's perfect standard. However, it does no good to look into a mirror if all we do is walk away, forgetting what we saw. When we study the Bible, we should do so with the intention of allowing it to transform us. Our goal is not to master it, but rather, to be mastered by it. Therefore, we should come to God's Word with two basic questions: 1) What does God want to say to me? and 2) What does God want me to do?

God's Word Demands Our Response

What is your response to God's Word? As Christians, we can know the Scriptures yet still not respond in obedience to what they are saying to us. By this, it is evident that we have not fully understood the truth. Below is a list of Scriptures that record some of the many responses Christians can have to the Word of God.

- Let it fall upon good ground in your heart: Mark 4:20
- Incline your heart to it: Psalm 119:36
- Hear it and do it to be wise: John 12:47
- Desire to have it established in your life: Psalm 119:38
- Keep the Word: John 14:23; Psalm 119:60
- Be willing to speak it before leaders: Psalm 119:46
- Let God's Word abide in you: John 5:38
- Meditate on it: Psalm 119:48
- Continue in His Word: John 8:31
- Walk according to its teachings: Psalm 119:59
- Not live only on physical food, but the Word: Matthew 4:4
- Praise His Word: Psalm 56:4
- Not forget it: Psalm 119:61
- Give thanks for it: Psalm 119:62

- Choose companions who also fear the Word: Psalm 119:63
- Magnify His Word even above His name: Psalm 138:2
- Engraft His Word in your heart: James 1:21
- Believe it: Psalm 119:66
- Be a doer of the Word and not a hearer only: James 1:22
- Desire the milk of His Word: 1 Peter 2:2
- Value it more than gold and silver: Psalm 119:72
- Let the Word of God dwell in you richly: Colossians 3:16
- Desire to learn it: Psalm 119:73
- Rightly divide the Word of God: 2 Timothy 2:15
- Hope in the Word: Psalm 119:74
- Search the Scriptures: John 5:39; Acts 17:11
- Do not forsake it: Psalm 119:87
- Find comfort in it: Psalm 119:76
- Choose His Word: Psalm 119:30
- Desire for it to change your heart: Psalm 119:80
- Stick to His Word: Psalm 119:31
- Run the way of His Word: Psalm 119:32
- Seek after it: Psalm 119:94
- Keep it: Psalm 119:33; Psalm 119:69
- Consider it: Psalm 119:95
- Observe it: Psalm 119:34
- Long for God's Word: Psalm 119:131
- Delight in it: Psalm 119:35
- Order your steps in the Word: Psalm 119:133
- Seek His precepts: Psalm 119:45
- Ask forgiveness for sin so His Word can abide in you: 1 John 1:10
- Be grieved when God's Word is not honored: Psalm 119:136
- Stand in awe of God's Word: Psalm 119:161
- Love it: Psalm 119:163
- Speak His Word: Psalm 119:172

chapter

02

Observation:
What Does It Say

Open my eyes, that I may see wondrous things from Your law.

—Psalm 119:18

I n the following chapters, we will review three basic skills that help us to understand and apply God's Word:

Chapter 2:	Observation—"See It" *What does it say?*
Chapter 3:	Interpretation—"Know It" *What does it mean?*
Chapter 4:	Application—"Do It" *What does it ask me to do?*

Every good study method incorporates these three basic principles. When we study the Bible in this way, we will discover the central truth of the passage and begin to build that truth into our daily lives.

"SEE IT"—Observe What the Text Is Actually Saying

To observe the passage means to take notice of it by fixing your mind upon the Scripture. In other words, don't just read it; carefully examine what it is saying. Observation demands time, concentration, and discipline. It cannot be hurried. The purpose of observation is to help you to see the context of the passage and absorb all of its meaning. The best way to do this is to simply read the passage a number of times, in a few different ways. For instance, first read it slowly and prayerfully, then once again aloud, and finally read it through, pausing at the end of each verse, and reflecting upon what it is saying. Each time you read the text be sure to write down everything you notice about the passage, even those things that seem obvious.

To Whom Was the Passage Written?

Although all Scripture was written for us, it wasn't all written to us. An important consideration when observing the text is determining who the original recipients would have been. This is necessary information in order to come to a correct understanding of the original meaning of any passage.

The Bible was written over a 1,500 year time span, and was primarily addressed to four general groups of people:

The Jews	The Church
The Gentiles	Individual Believers

Keywords and Phrases

Identifying keywords and phrases helps unlock the meaning of a biblical passage. Keywords are usually those that are used repeatedly throughout the text. They are vital to the understanding of the context, and would strip the passage of its central meaning if they were removed. Keywords and phrases can include pronouns, synonyms, and any related words or phrases. After identifying the keywords and phrases in the text, you will be able to discern the main subject(s); this in turn will reveal the theme— unifying idea—of the chapter or book.

KEYWORDS/PHRASES > MAIN SUBJECTS > OVERALL THEME

Put Yourself in the Picture

Pastor Skip Heitzig said, "One technique has helped me study the Scripture more than any other single thing, and that is trying to place myself into the text. By picturing the scene and getting behind the words, I begin to see things, as they were when the author was inspired to write them. I ask myself to who was the letter or book addressed; what problems were they facing; what was the purpose of the writing; and other questions as they occur to me. Then I place myself in the crowd. I'm wearing an ancient tunic and I'm traveling towards Jerusalem. Suddenly, my curiosity compels me to find out why a crowd has gathered down by the Jordan River." Reading the Scriptures as though you are a part of the scene is exciting and brings the story to life. Try it!

The Five W's

As you read remember the five W's: **who, what, when, where,** and **why.** Answering these questions from the text will help you see the bigger picture. For instance:

1. **Who**: Who are the people in the story? Who is writing? Who is being written to: Jews, Gentiles, or the Church?

2. **What**: What is being communicated? What is happening? What caused it to happen? What feelings are involved?

3. **When**: When did it happen? When will it happen? When did they find out?

4. **Where**: Where are they going? Where did it happen? Where did they come from? Where will it take place?

5. **Why**: Why did he say that? Why did he do that? Why did he go there? Why is it important?

Keep Asking Questions

A good sleuth picks up clues others miss by interrogating those involved and questioning the facts of the case. The same can be said of Bible study. Questions are invaluable to learning what is going on in any passage. I've listed some good investigative questions below. You can use these, or come up with some of your own. The point is: ask lots of questions.

1. Does the passage contain any repeated words or phrases?

2. Does the passage raise or answer any questions?

3. Does the passage present a problem and/or a solution?

4. What, if anything, do I not understand?

5. What is the tone of the passage?

6. Does the text contain any commands, warnings, or promises?

7. What contrasts or comparisons exist in the passage?

8. What illustrations does the writer use?

9. Do you notice a progression from the general to the specific?

10. Is there a list given in the passage?

11. Is advice being given and/or received?

12. What are the Bible characters attitudes?

13. Are any Old Testament quotes used in a New Testament passage?

14. What powerful verbs are being used in the passage?
    (I.e., transformed, justified, interceded, etc.)

15. Does anything unusual stick out to you about the passage?

16. What truths or facts are being implied or inferred?

The Major Theme of the Bible

If someone were to ask you what the major theme of the Bible is, would you know the answer? If you said that the major theme of the Bible is redemption, you would be correct. In the Old Testament there is the anticipation of it in type and prophecy; in the gospels, the accomplishment of it by the death and resurrection of Christ; in Acts and the epistles, the application of it to the needs of man; and in the Revelation, the achievement of it in the subjection of all kingdoms to the rule of God. Each and every part of the Bible, whether history, literature, type, prophecy, law, or grace, is part of the design of God to reconcile to Himself, by the sacrifice of Himself, a fallen and rebellious race.

John MacArthur says that within the Bible's main theme of redemption five additional subcategories or sub-themes exist:

1. The nature of God.

2. The curse for sin and disobedience.

3. The blessing for faith and obedience.

4. The Lord, our Savior, and the sacrifice for sin.

5. The coming kingdom and glory.

25

As we study the Scriptures, it is essential to understand that these recurring sub-themes are the hooks upon which we hang every passage. We can relate each portion of Scripture to one or more of these topics by asking the question: "Into which subcategory does this Scripture fit?"

Overlooking Biblical Facts Is Easy

Good students of God's Word are those who have simply trained themselves to observe things in the text that others overlook. Important biblical facts are often missed for one of the following three reasons:

1. We rush through a passage too quickly. Slow down.

2. We don't write down our observations. Louis Agassiz, a professor of zoology at Harvard used to teach his students the art of observation by saying, "A pencil is the best eye." If you want to remember it...write it down.

3. We give up too soon. The longer you squeeze an orange, the more juice you get out of it. Eventually an orange runs out of juice, but the Bible never runs dry. You can study a text dozens of times and still squeeze more meaning out of it. So, don't give up too soon.

Pay Attention to Figures of Speech

Being aware of what literary style is being used by the writer is necessary to the understanding of the passage. The following list contains some of the most common figures of speech found in the Scriptures, which help us to define its style:

Comparison (A resemblance is shown between two different things.)
- Psalm 84:10: "For a day in Your courts is better than a thousand. I would rather be a doorkeeper in the house of my God than dwell in the tents of wickedness."
- Other Examples: James 3:3-6; Matthew 12:11-12

Contrast (Two things set in opposition to one another.)
- Proverbs 11:1: "Dishonest scales are an abomination to the LORD, but a just weight is His delight."
- Other Examples: James 2:2-4; 3:12; 2 Corinthians 3:5-6; Matthew 6:24; Romans 6:23

<u>Simile</u> (One thing is likened to another by direct statement.)

- Psalm 103:11: "For as the heavens are high above the earth, so great is His mercy toward those who fear Him"
- Other Verses: Psalm 1:3; 44:22; Proverbs 25:25

<u>Metaphor</u> (One thing is likened to another by implication.)

- Ephesians 2:20: "...built on the foundation of the apostles and prophets, Jesus Christ Himself being the chief cornerstone"
- Other Verses: Colossians 1:18; John 6:48; 10:9; 15:5; 1 John 1:5; Proverbs 20:27

<u>Allegory</u> (Similar to a parable, but with a possible literal interpretation.)

- Judges 9:7-15: Jotham's allegory of the trees that sought a king.
- Other Verses: Psalm 80:8-16; Isaiah 5:1-7; Ezekiel 17; John 10:1-18; Revelation 17

<u>Personification</u> (Attributing human qualities to inanimate objects.)

- Psalm 19:1-4: "The heavens declare the glory of God; and the firmament shows His handiwork. Day unto day utters speech, and night unto night reveals knowledge...."
- Other Verses: Proverbs 1:20; 2:1-9

<u>Hyperbole</u> (Use of exaggerated terms for emphasis.)

- Matthew 16:26: "For what profit is it to a man if he gains the whole world, and loses his own soul?"
- Other Verses: Matthew 5:29; John 21:25; 2 Chronicles 36:23

<u>Type</u> (When one thing supplies a suggestion or forecast of another.)

- Romans 5:14: "...death reigned from Adam to Moses, even over those who had not sinned according to the likeness of the transgression of Adam, who is a type of Him who was to come."
- Other Verses: 1 Corinthians 15:45; Revelation 21:2; 22:17; Matthew 25:1

Irony (An incongruity between the intended meaning of an action and its actual meaning.)

- Matthew 7:3: "And why do you look at the speck in your brother's eye, but do not consider the plank in your own eye?"
- Other Verses: 2 Samuel 6:20; 1 Kings 18:27; Job 12:2; Amos 4:4

Apostrophe (An exclamatory passage towards an absent individual.)

- 1 Corinthians 15:55: "O Death, where is your sting? O Hades, where is your victory?"
- Other Verses: Isaiah 51:9; Amos 4:1

Anthropomorphisms (Attributing a physical human behavior to God.)

- 2 Chronicles 16:9: "For the eyes of the Lord run to and fro throughout the whole earth..."
- Other Verses: Exodus 3:20; 32:14; Isaiah 38:1-5; Genesis 6:6; Numbers 11:25

Anthropopathisms (Describing God as displaying human emotions.)

- Exodus 20:5: "For I, the Lord your God, am a jealous God..."
- Psalm 103:8: "The Lord is merciful and gracious, slow to anger, and abounding in mercy."

Synecdoche (A part is made to stand for a whole, or a whole for a part.)

- Romans 3:25: "whom God set forth as a propitiation by His blood, through faith ...." (For His completed work.)
- Other Verses: 1 Corinthians 1:22; Revelation 1:11

Observation is a skill that is developed by slowing down and carefully reading the Scriptures. When we set out to observe the text we will see more of its meaning. This is the first step in learning how to study the Bible. In the next chapter, we will be looking at what it means to correctly interpret all that we observe in the text.

chapter

03

Interpretation:
What Does It Mean?

*The natural man does not receive the things of the Spirit of God,
for they are foolishness to him; nor can he know them, because
they are spiritually discerned.*

—1 Corinthians 2:14

E very good Bible study method has as one of its main objectives, the
correct interpretation of the Scriptures. However, Dr. Roy B. Zuck,
of Dallas Theological Seminary says, "Most of the time when many
people approach the Bible, they jump from observation to application,
skipping the essential step of interpretation. This is wrong because interpretation logically follows observation. In observing what the Bible says,
you probe; in interpretation, you mull. Observation is discovery; interpretation is digesting. Observation means looking at what is there, and
interpretation is deciding what it means. The one is to explore, the other
is to explain." In the previous chapter, we looked at how sharpening our
observation skills can help us *see* the text more clearly. In this chapter,
we are going to discover how the right interpretation of God's Word turns
what we "see" into what we "know."

"KNOW IT"—Interpretation Helps Us Discover the Meaning

A correct interpretation of Scripture will never be discerned strictly by
human logic. We cannot simply apply our intellect to the text; we must be
willing to allow the revealed wisdom of God to speak to us through the

pages of Scripture. Many Christians miss the truth of God's Word because they are trying to mold its precepts to fit their own personal ideologies. They read meaning into the text rather than drawing understanding from it. However, when we come to the Bible prepared to have our thoughts and ideas conformed to its authority (rather than the other way around) then whether we are seasoned biblical scholars or the youngest Sunday school students we will be able to come away with a correct understanding. The best assurance we have of arriving at the right interpretation of any biblical passage always begins with laying aside our own preconceived notions, gut feelings, long-held beliefs, and persuasive arguments, and allowing the Word of God and the Spirit of God to impart understanding to us.

The Bible is the ultimate authority in the church and in the lives of individual believers. However, people often discredit the Bible with comments such as, "Well, everyone has their own understanding of what the Bible means," or "there are as many interpretations of the Bible as there are Christians." But statements such as these are simply untrue. 2 Peter 1:20-21 reminds us that the Word of God has only one correct interpretation: "No prophecy of Scripture is of any private interpretation, for prophecy never came by the will of man, but holy men of God spoke as they were moved by the Holy Spirit."

We should never approach the Bible in the same subjective way in which we would view a painting by Picasso. The Bible is not an abstract piece of art that invites everyone to weigh in with his or her own opinion of it's meaning. Every passage of Scripture has an intended and discoverable truth—one correct interpretation.

As with observation, some obvious questions can be asked that will help us come to the correct interpretation of the writer's original intent:

1. Why did the writer say this?
2. What is the meaning of this?
3. What is the significance of this?
4. What is the implication of this?
5. Why is this important?

Prayer is also a key factor in assuring that we always come to a correct understanding of the Scriptures. In fact, when it comes to God's Word I believe prayer is even more valuable than seminary. The richness of every biblical passage will be revealed to those who read the Bible on their knees.

How Does the Passage Relate to the Whole Bible?

Never divorce one part of Scripture from another. The interpretation of every text must be consistent and coherent with the Bible as a whole. A. T. Pierson said that a "Partial examination will result in partial views of truth, which are necessarily imperfect; only careful comparison will show the complete mind of God." When we read the Bible, we must do so with great discernment and test every teaching by the whole of Scripture. This is called correlation: the process of relating one passage to another. Weighing the Scriptures in this manner will help prevent unbalanced and erroneous interpretations.

What Is the Context?

The context of the passage is the setting in which it "dwells." In simple terms, to read a passage in context means to view it in light of the surrounding verses—the "neighbors" so to speak. In order to assess the full meaning of any verse it must be read in its context. Just as a fish doesn't do well if you take it out of water, when a passage of Scripture is taken out of its proper context it loses its meaning. So, whenever you are studying a chapter or verse the first rule of establishing context is to know the book's overall theme.

Biblical exegesis (or interpretation of specific texts) is the process that enables us, as twenty-first century readers, to understand the original meaning of the ancient writings. A good exegesis of a passage of Scripture attempts to reveal what the writer originally intended to communicate and why. One way to do this is by tracing the "thread of thought" from where the writer first introduced an idea and tracking it all the way to its conclusion. Doing this connects the passage being studied with its broader context within the whole of Scripture and the intended meaning becomes apparent. One reformed theologian, Ulrich Zwingli, emphasized the importance of studying Scripture in context declaring that pulling a passage out of context "is like breaking off a flower from its roots."

Determining context requires that a passage be examined to answer these two questions:

1. <u>What is the historical setting</u>? The time and culture in which the writer and his readers lived, has a bearing on the interpretation of the passage. This includes the geographical, topographical, and

political environment, as well as the occasion and purpose of the book, letter, psalm, or prophetic oracle.

2. <u>What is the literary setting</u>? This means that 1) individual words derive meaning from the sentence, and 2) biblical sentences for the most part only have clear meaning in relation to the preceding and succeeding sentences. So, ask: What's the point being made? What is the writer saying? Why does he say it right now? How does it relate to what was just said? How does it relate to what's said next?

We will avoid a great deal of misinterpretation by remembering to check the context of a verse. Here are a few basic questions that will help you to determine the context of a biblical passage:

- Who is speaking?
- Who is being spoken to?
- When is it being spoken?
- Where is it being spoken?
- What is the occasion or circumstance?
- What is the main subject of the message?
- Is the meaning of what is being said revealed?
- What other background material clarifies this statement?

Cross-References Further Understanding

A puritan writer exhorted believers to, "Compare Scripture with Scripture." He said, "False doctrines, like false witnesses, agree not among themselves." In the same way that trapeze artists performing on the high-wire are protected by a net below, which catches them in the event of a fall, comparing Scripture with Scripture provides a doctrinal "safety net" to keep the interpreter from falling into an inconsistent understanding or interpretation. Donald Grey Barnhouse said, "You very rarely have to go outside the Bible to explain anything in the Bible." The beauty of using Scripture to interpret Scripture is that when the Bible answers its own questions, we know the answer is correct. Why? Because God never contradicts Himself—the Bible is unified in its message. Although it sometimes presents us with a paradox, it never confounds us with a contradiction. Puritan writer Thomas Watson wisely stated, "Nothing can cut the diamond but the diamond; nothing can interpret Scripture but Scripture." But how do you know which Scriptures to compare?

1. Look up any related verses that come to mind as you read.

2. Use the cross-references in the margin of your Bible.

3. The *Treasury of Scripture Knowledge* is a helpful resource.

These next two principles offer possible clarification, but they are not laws. You will definitely find exceptions to them, but they can often be helpful to those who want to come to a better understanding of Scripture.

1. The Principle of First Mention:
   The general principle of first mention says that the first time a word, phrase, object, or incident is mentioned in the Bible provides a key to its meaning throughout the rest of Scripture. For example, in Genesis 3 there is the first mention of fig leaves. Adam used fig leaves to try to cover his sin and nakedness. The fig leaves represented his attempt to justify himself before God. They carry the same meaning throughout the rest of Scripture. For example, in Matthew 21 the fig tree represents the self-righteous nation of Israel who was trying to be righteous through self-efforts.

2. The Principle of Repetition:
   All Scripture is divinely inspired. Each word in the original manuscript is God-breathed and purposed. For this reason, when something is repeated in Scripture it is done so, intentionally, for special emphasis. It means that the truth that is being expressed is of such importance that it needs to be repeated. One example is the repetition of the phrase "born again" in John 3:3, 5, and 7. Remember: repetition is the Holy Spirit's way of saying, "Stop and look again."

When All Else Fails Try a Commentary

Commentaries are great tools to enrich our study of God's Word. However, never let reading a commentary take the place of doing your own study. Generally, you should try not to refer to a commentary until after you have completed your own observation and interpretation. Don't let anything rob you of the joy of discovering rich biblical insights yourself. But once you have done that, commentaries are helpful in answering those questions that you were unable to find answers to on your own. God has given many gifted teachers to the church throughout the years, so if you are stuck, find a good commentary and continue studying until you have a full understanding of the passage. Visit our website at http://www.learntostudythe-bible.com for a list of recommended commentaries.

chapter
04

Application:
What Does It Ask Me To Do?

He who looks into the perfect law of liberty and continues in it,
and is not a forgetful hearer but a doer of the work, this one will
be blessed in what he does.

—James 1:25

Application puts feet on our Bible study—we cannot really say we know the truth until we walk in it. Dr. Roy B. Zuck said, "Heart appropriation, not merely head apprehension, is the true goal of Bible study." In this chapter, we will be focusing on the ultimate aim of every Bible study method: a transformed life. It is impossible to study the Scriptures diligently without running headfirst into the need for personal application. When we know what a passage means (interpretation), we are responsible to put what we know into practice (application). As we "do it," our lives are transformed.

"DO IT"—Are You Applying What You Know?

How do we apply the Bible to our daily lives? Simple. We become "doers of the Word." James 1:22 says that if we are hearers only we are deceiving ourselves. God's purpose for our study time is transformation—He wants to make us more like Jesus. He is not impressed by our knowledge; He is blessed by our obedience. So one very important question that we need to be asking as we study the Bible is how can we apply what we are learning to our lives each day.

The greatest evidence that we love God is that we walk in obedience to His Word, not out of a sense of duty or in response to a book of rules, but out of a genuine heart of love and devotion to Him. Love for God will always motivate us to obey His commands and seek to glorify Him in every area of our lives. An unwillingness to apply the Scriptures to our lives will inevitably lead to spiritual insensitivity to the Lord and to His people. If a Christian is careless in Bible reading, he will care less about Christian living.

Indeed, applying the Bible to our lives changes the way we think, act, and live. As Ralph Waldo Emerson wrote: "Sow a thought and you reap an action; sow an act and you reap a habit; sow a habit and you reap a character; sow a character, and you reap a destiny!" Perhaps W. H. Griffith described it best of all when he said, "Through and above all stages we must press until we arrive at the summit, which is the use of the Bible as God's personal Word to our own souls, 'What saith my Lord unto His servant?' 'What wilt Thou have me to do?' The Scriptures are intended to lead the soul directly to God, to introduce it to His presence, and to convey His revelation of truth and grace. And if we fail to realize this, we fail at the critical point, and all our other knowledge, great and valuable though it be, will count for little or nothing."

Do Not Neglect Application

Remember, observation, interpretation, and application work together in transforming the way we live our lives. Each stage in the process is necessary, however application is both the most needed and the most neglected of them all. It is truly better to live one verse of the Bible than to recite an entire chapter from memory. Don't be deceived! Every time we hear the Word of God, we choose whether we will obey it. Oswald Chambers said, "One step forward in obedience is worth years of study about it." It is possible to have heads that are filled with Scripture and yet have hearts and lives that are filled with carnality. Every Bible should come with the following label:

> Warning: This Book is habit-forming. Regular use causes loss of anxiety, and a decreased desire to lie, cheat, steal, or hate. Common side effects may include: increased sensations of love, peace, joy, and compassion.

The Three P's of Good Application

- Personal: Ask yourself: How does this truth apply to my life? (At work? At home? At school?) Make it personal by writing your answers in the first person singular, using the personal pronouns "I," "my," and "mine" as you record your thoughts.

- Practical: Ask yourself: In view of this truth, what specific changes should l make in my life? It ought to be something that you can begin doing right away. Plan a definite course of action and begin to implement it. Design a practical project, which will encourage you to be a "doer of the Word." Make your application as specific as possible. Broad generalities will leave you feeling helpless and produce little action.

- Provable: Ask yourself: How do I propose to carry out these changes? When will I do this? Be specific in determining the answers to these questions. Set up some sort of follow-up to check your progress. It has to be measurable so you can know that you have done it. It is also good to set a deadline for your application.

What Are Some Possible Applications?

Application depends on the Scripture you are studying. Your application will come from the correct interpretation of the Scriptures you are reading, so to aid you in thinking about possible applications remember this little acronym: **SPACE PETS**—silly, yes but it will help you as you look for ways to apply what you are studying and learning to your daily life.

S - Is there a **Sin** to avoid, forsake, or confess?

P - Is there a **Promise** to believe and conditions to meet?

A - Is there an **Attitude** to change or an **Action** to take?

C - Is there a **Command** to keep?

E - Is there an **Example** to follow?

P - Is there a **Prayer** to pray or a **Priority** to change?

E - Is there an **Error** to mark?

T - Is there a **Truth** to meditate upon?

S - Is there a **Specific** thing to thank God for?

Other Possible Applications Include:

• Memorizing an impressive biblical truth.	• Doing a kindness anonymously for someone.
• Doing a special Bible study on the topic.	• Giving a gift to a friend, or an enemy.
• Writing a letter of apology or encouragement to someone in your life.	• Building relationships with both God and others (family and friends).
• Righting a wrong that you have committed.	• Making a change to your schedule.

The point is, be specific on the ways in which God's Word is directing your actions, and do it quickly. Don't delay! You can stand in an ice-cream shop all day long and stare at all the flavors, but no enjoyment or satisfaction will come until you bite into a scoop for yourself. What is your response to God's Word? How have you responded in the past? Whatever action is needed in your life today, are you willing to do it? Be as specific as you can and make sure you follow through. Be accountable to someone; ask a friend or family member to help you get it done.

Not Everything Applies Equally

Some of the material in the Bible is not directly applicable to us, today. For example, all the people of Israel were ordered to appear three times a year before the Lord in Jerusalem for major Jewish festivals. We obviously do not need to do that. But we can ask ourselves how a command such as this, which was given to God's people before Jesus came, encourages us to be faithful in what we are called to do today (i.e. attend church, and have regular private times of devotion). True, we do not have to travel to Israel to meet with the Lord, but how often are we meeting with Him based on the means He has established for us?

More Verses Apply Than We Think

Imagine stumbling across this verse in your time of morning devotions, "Do not muzzle an ox while it is treading out the grain" (Deuteronomy 25:4). Now, if you happen to be a farmer who uses oxen, this could be an exciting moment for you. But, what about the rest of us who are not farmers, how can we find an application in this verse? In 1 Corinthians

9:7-9, Paul realized that this command about an ox was a specific illustration that could be applied to a broader principle; namely that animals and people have a right to be paid for their work. The way that Paul handled this verse gives us a model for how we can apply seemingly outdated and irrelevant Scriptures to our daily lives. To come to a correct application of a specific passage such as this, we can follow these same guidelines:

1. Understand the original situation and how God's Word applied to that situation (the oxen had a right to eat).

2. Determine whether God's Word in that situation reflects a specific application or a broader principle. (In this case the broader principle is that those who work have a right to be paid.)

3. Apply the broader principle to the situations you are facing (in Paul's case it was that a minister had a right to be paid for his work too).

Learning how to look beyond the specifics of a particular biblical text in order to deduce its more generalized implications, is one of the most important steps in applying the Bible. When on the surface a passage of Scripture seems to have little to do with our situation today, we need to search out the broader principle that is being conveyed. The broader context usually will reveal a general principle that can be applied to our lives. Reflecting upon the timeless qualities of the Bible helps us to see and know how to apply it in whatever situation we face. Whenever any key elements in your situation compares to the specifics of the original, then you can safely apply the general principle, as long as it doesn't contradict God's Word elsewhere.

Be alert for the following deceptive dangers regarding application:

1. Substituting interpretation for application.
   Remember, knowing it and doing it is not the same thing.

2. Substituting a one-time obedience for a substantial life-change.

3. Substituting rationalization of your sin for repentance from it.

Application Is Never Accidental

Application takes work. Unless we determine to apply the Scriptures to our lives, we never will. Three things that often hinder us from applying what we are learning in God's Word are:

1. <u>Laziness</u>: Application is difficult because it requires thinking. Sometimes it takes a long period of meditation (concentrated, prayerful thinking) before we see a way to apply a Bible truth.

2. <u>Spiritual Warfare</u>: Application is hard because Satan fights it, he doesn't want our lives to affect others for the Lord. The Devil's strongest attack often comes as we are seeking to apply what we have studied.

3. <u>Selfishness</u>: Application is hard because it goes against our natural tendencies. Change is often unwelcome in our lives. We don't like it, it is uncomfortable and not our choosing. But change is what true application requires. If we allow our choices to be driven by our emotions and feelings, rather than by our determined will, we are resisting the transforming work that God wants to do and choosing to stay the way we are.

Living Epistles

Martin Luther said, "The world does not need a definition of religion as much as it needs a demonstration." That demonstration comes when we begin to be doers of the Word. In the margin of many pages in D. L. Moody's Bible, he wrote the letters T and P, (tried and proved) next to every passage that he had personally tried and proved, in his life. A.T. Pierson speaking about the Bible, said, "While other books inform, and a few reform, this one Book transforms." What are you doing with His Word? Are you the Christian who reads the Bible but doesn't apply it? Don't be deceived—obedience is the key to living a transformed and powerful Christian life.

Keep an Application Journal

As you are reading your Bible each day, it is helpful to keep track of the applications that you desire to make. A simple journal will help you keep tabs on how you are doing. Record your application goals on a daily or weekly basis and review them periodically to see how many of them you have actually followed through on. This notebook will prove to be the most helpful Bible study tool you will ever have because it will show you how much or how little you are applying what you are reading. God has given us the potential to live transformed lives for Him, but we must choose to make the changes necessary each day, to accomplish what He desires for us. One thing is certain: Our lives will change as we consistently apply the Scriptures we are reading. On the next page is a sample chart you can use.

Application Journal Chart

Date	Scripture	Application Goal	Deadline	Completed *

* Include in this column how you or someone else was blessed when you were faithful to apply the Scriptures practically. This will serve as a reminder to you to continue working at being a doer of the Word.

chapter

05

How to Have Daily Devotions

He Himself often withdrew into the wilderness and prayed.

—Luke 5:16

One of the greatest applications we can make from studying God's Word is a decision to set aside time each day for personal devotions. The purpose of this time is simply to quiet our hearts before the Lord and have fellowship with Him. Our daily devotions are not meant to be a time of in-depth Bible study. During your quiet time, plan to simply draw closer to the Lord through meditation on His Word and communion with Him in prayer. In this chapter, we are going to focus on some of the essentials that go into planning a daily devotion time that will help us be more deliberate about enjoying Jesus' presence, every day.

> **NOTE**: *Daily devotions are an opportunity to enjoy God's presence. An attitude that daily devotions are "nice but not necessary" isn't going to help you be consistent. You must make it a non-negotiable priority, otherwise you may sell yourself short on experiencing abundant life.*

Why Have Daily Devotions?

- God created people in His image for the purpose of fellowship (Genesis 1:26). Humans are the only created beings that have the capacity for intimate fellowship with the One who created them.

When Adam sinned, fellowship between man and God was lost, but when Jesus Christ died and rose again, He restored the possibility for man to have fellowship with God. All who believe in Jesus have the privilege of enjoying a personal relationship with the Father (1 Corinthians 1:9; 1 John 1:3-4).

- <u>Jesus' quiet time was a source of His strength</u>. Personal fellowship with His Father in heaven was a top priority of Jesus' life on earth (Mark 1:35; Luke 5:16; 22:39-44). Even when His days were filled with exciting ministry, He spent time in prayer (John 5:30). If a time of quiet prayer was a priority for Jesus, how much more do we need to make it a priority in our lives?

- <u>Have you ever gone without food for a day</u>? If so, you know how quickly hunger sets in. And if you go without food for too long, your strength will begin to diminish. The same is true in our spiritual lives. The Bible is our soul's food. It is a sign of health for a Christian to have an appetite for the Word of God. It is the only way that we will be well nourished and spiritually strong. Yet, many Christians consistently try to get by with only one meal a week—Sunday morning. You could not survive long, physically, if all you were eating was one meal a week, and neither can you make it spiritually, on such small portions of God's Word.

- <u>How long would you go without bathing</u>? A daily quiet time is like a spiritual bath (Ephesians 5:26; John 15:3). We wouldn't have many friends if we went for long periods without bathing. The Bible says that reading the Word of God is what cleanses us—our lives will begin to stink if we neglect the Word.

- <u>We gain tremendous rewards from having a quiet time</u>. The final reason we should have a daily quiet time is the tremendous results it brings into our lives. God has promised many things to those who take the time to get to know him through His Word and prayer. Some of the rewards of having a daily quiet time include:

Joy (Psalm 16:11)	Success (Joshua 1:8)
Strength (Isaiah 40:29-31)	Answered prayer (John 15:7)
Peace (Psalm 119:165)	Personal testimony (Acts 4:13)

The Privilege of Meeting With God

During our quiet times, we have the privilege of meeting with God—we get direction from Him, gain delight in Him, and become more like Jesus as we sit quietly in His presence. In our personal time of fellowship with the Creator, we reap the following benefits:

- <u>An opportunity to worship God</u>: The first benefit of time spent quietly with the Lord each day, is that it allows us to give to God instead of getting from Him. Psalm 29:2 says, "Give unto the LORD the glory due to His name; worship the LORD in the beauty of holiness." Many Christians overemphasize their work for God and neglect to spend time simply worshipping Him. God deserves and desires our devotion (John 4:23). How long has it been since you sat quietly with Jesus and simply told Him that you love Him? When was the last time you sang a worship song to Him outside of a church service?

- <u>We get direction from God</u>: The second benefit of our quiet time with the Lord is that we get direction from Him for our daily lives (Psalm 25:4-5; 40:8). When we sit quietly with the Lord it gives us the opportunity to hear from God and to get the wisdom and direction we need. In our fast-paced world, we desperately need to slow down and hear from the One who knows the end from the beginning. Pascal once said, "All the troubles of man arise from his inability to sit still." Ask God to show you His will for your day and commit your schedule to Him.

- <u>We gain delight in God</u>: The third benefit of our personal time with the Lord is enjoying Him and basking in His presence. The secret of real joy comes from knowing God (Psalm 34:8; Philippians 3:10). Do you know Jesus Christ personally, or do you merely know about Him? When we know a person intimately, we:

  1. Spend quality time together.

  2. Enjoy meaningful communication.

  3. Know what each others likes and dislikes are.

When we expect to meet with Jesus during our quiet time each morning we will never be disappointed. We will always find that He's waiting to meet with us too.

- <u>We become more Christ-like</u>: How do we become more like Jesus? We are made holy through the Word (John 17:17; Romans 12:2). Our sanctification comes directly through the time we spend in the Scriptures getting to know God intimately, and allowing His Word to correct our hearts.

No Time to Pray!

We often make the excuse that we are too busy to pray, but the truth is we all have exactly the same amount of time each week—168 hours—and we spend that time on the things we think are important. So, it's not a matter of having enough time, but of having the right priorities on how we spend our time. What is important to you? When we put God first, He will multiply our time and efficiency (Matthew 6:33). So, don't let anything rob you from spending time with Jesus. Preserve it at all cost. Someone once said, "If you want to find out what a man is really like, find out what he is like alone with God." Martin Luther, the father of the Reformation is quoted as having said, "I have so much to do today that I must spend at least three hours in prayer." The busier he was, the more he prayed. If you are too busy to have daily devotions, then you are too busy, period. We must simplify our lives or we will lose untold treasures from God.

How Do We Have Powerful Daily Devotions?

A script cannot be written for our quiet times with the Lord. We can be as close to Him each day as we choose to be. He delights in our desire to simply be with Him. So, while I am not going to give you five easy steps to planning a successful quiet time with Jesus, what I do have to offer are some general suggestions that you can prayerfully consider as you sit before the Lord.

1. <u>Begin with the Right Attitude</u>

If you have been spending a lot of time dealing with hectic schedules or anxieties over your business or family life, you cannot expect to pick up the Bible and immediately enter into its heavenly mysteries. Just as you ask a blessing over your meal before you eat it, so to, it is a good rule to ask the Lord to bless you as you partake of this heavenly food. If you don't take the time to pray before opening God's Word, it is completely possible that even though you are doing the right thing—reading the Bible—you will be doing it with the wrong attitude. Begin your time with God in prayer and you will have the right attitude:

- Expectancy: You will expect to have a good time of fellowship.

- Reverence: Your heart will be prepared and still before His Majesty.

- Alertness: You will give Him your best.

- Teachability: You will come for the purpose of doing what God asks.

2. Choose a Consistent Time

Always give God the best part of your day. Make sure you are consistent with that time, and that it is free from as many interruptions as possible. Don't try to squeeze the Lord into your already tight schedule, have a plan that provides a set time—put it on your calendar if necessary. For most of us, early in the morning usually works best. In fact, Jesus often chose to pray and meet alone with the Father early in the morning (Mark 1:35) and so did king David (Psalm 5:3). Time spent with the Father is more important than an extra hour of sleep. Pioneer missionary Hudson Taylor once said, "You don't tune up the instruments after the concert is over." How true! It's logical to tune your instruments before you start to play. The same is true for our spiritual lives. If Jesus is really in first place, we ought to give him the first part of the day. After all, doctors tell us that the most important meal of the day is breakfast because it determines our energy levels, alertness, and even our moods. Likewise, we also need a "spiritual breakfast." When we start the day with the Word of God, we are beginning on a high note. We will often be able to share what we receive in the morning as an encouragement to others throughout the day.

However, whether you choose to spend time with the Lord in the morning, afternoon, or evening, remember:

1. Be consistent—make an appointment with God.

2. Look forward to it.

3. Don't stand Him up.

You might even consider having two quiet times (morning and evening). Stephen Olford, a well-known pastor once said, "I want to hear the voice of God before I hear anyone else's in the morning, and His is the last voice I want to hear at night."

45

3. How Much Time Should We Spend With the Lord?

Aim to spend not less than fifteen minutes a day with God in your personal devotions. Out of the 168 hours we all have in a week that will only take, one hour and forty-five minutes of your weekly routine. That seems terribly small when you consider that you were created to have meaningful fellowship with God. Here's a helpful hint: Watching the clock will ruin your time with God, instead try setting an alarm.

4. Choose a Consistent Location

Jesus had a custom of praying in the quiet garden of Gethsemane on the Mount of Olives (Luke 22:39). The place you choose ought to be a quiet and secluded place where you can be alone and undisturbed. In today's noisy world this may take some ingenuity, but it is important. As you consistently meet with the Lord in that place, it will become special because of the wonderful times you have had with Jesus.

5. Practice True Reading

Do you read the Bible in a hurried way: Just a little tidbit and off you go? Do you soon forget what you have read? Do you quickly lose what little effect it had upon you? Be resolved to get at its soul, its juice, its life, its essence, and to drink in its meaning. If you don't read carefully enough to understand than your reading is a dead reading and is unprofitable. In C. H. Spurgeon's sermon "How to Read the Bible" he speaks of some people who comfort themselves with the idea that they have done a good action when they have read a chapter of the Bible, even though the meaning of it has not been found by them. Nature itself rejects this as ridiculous. If you had turned the book upside down and spent the same time looking at the different characters you would have gained as much good from it as you will reading it right side up without understanding it. You will never get comfort for your soul out of what you do not understand, nor find guidance for your life out of what you do not comprehend. Understanding the meaning is the essence of true reading. With some people they can read a very great deal, because they do not read anything. The eye glances but the mind never rests. The soul does not discover the truth and stay there long enough. Such reading is not reading at all. If reading is a mechanical exercise it profits nothing.

If you are to understand what you read, you will need to meditate upon it. This simply means to carefully and slowly consider what you have read until you fully understand what God is speaking to you from that passage of Scripture. There are certain texts, which almost seem to be designed, purposely, to make you think. The diligence of the heart in seeking to know the Divine Mind, in such instances, does more good than vast knowledge that is easily found. So press forward to understanding! Heavenly gold is worth digging for, but you are not likely to discover it unless you spend the time meditating on Scripture.

6. <u>Have a Basic Plan</u>

It's been said, "If you aim at nothing, you are sure to hit it!" To have a meaningful quiet time, you will need some general guidelines to follow. It could be something as simple as:

- <u>Briefly Pray</u>: Invite Jesus to be with you (Psalm 139:23-24).

- <u>Praise God</u>: Read a Psalm out loud or sing a praise song to get your heart and spirit in an attitude of worship.

- <u>Read the Bible</u>: Read slowly and systematically (not randomly), and read only a small portion. If you follow a Bible in a year reading plan, after you have finished your assigned reading for the day choose a small portion of it and review it more devotionally.

- <u>Meditate</u>: You can meditate on Scripture by reading the passage out loud a few times, asking questions, memorizing a verse, reading in a couple of different translations, paraphrasing it in your own words, and so forth. Talk with God about how this verse relates to your life and how He wants you to practically apply this truth.

- <u>Journal</u>: Write down any key thoughts the Lord gives you.

- <u>Close in Prayer</u>: After God has spoken His Word to you; speak to Him. Include times of adoration, worship, thanksgiving, confession, intercession, and petition. Occasionally vary your physical positions in prayer (kneeling/standing). Tell God how you desire to respond to Him today.

7. <u>Vary Your Plan Often</u>

Guard yourself from routine. Any good relationship is built on a variety of activities and experiences, and the same holds true with your relationship with God. Maybe you should spend the whole time in prayer or song, maybe one day you can walk as you read and pray, or maybe you should write a letter to God expressing your heart for Him instead of your normal journaling. However you mix it up, keep it exciting—don't let your devotions become a duty. Never become devoted to the habit—only to the Savior. J. Wilbur Chapman wrote this about the core components of his quiet time:

- Study it through: Never begin a day without mastering a Bible verse. Ask God to help you focus on a specific verse within the passage you are reading.

- Pray it in: Never lay aside your Bible until the verse or passage you have studied has become a part of your being. Meditate.

- Put it down: Record any thoughts that God gives you in the margin of your Bible or in your notebook or journal. Writing is key!

- Work it out: Live out the truth you receive in the morning through each hour of the day. Don't let your day end without applying Scripture.

8. Read With the Purpose of Meeting With Jesus

Some read the Bible from cover to cover, and yet it remains a dead book. When you are reading the Scriptures ask the Lord to help you grasp the truth of how much greater His Word is, than just the inanimate book that you are holding in your hands. Specifically, that you would see Jesus Himself in all you read. When His presence illuminates His Word, it comes alive: He leans over you, He runs His finger along the lines, He breaths life into every Word, and His pierced hand begins directing your heart. Those who read to meet with Jesus, find the soul of Scripture. Indeed, if He is not found in the Scriptures, they will be of small service: For what did Jesus say? "You search the Scriptures, for in them you think you have eternal life; and these are they which testify of Me" (John 5:39). Cling to the Scripture, for it is in them that you will see Jesus.

9. Each Day Have a Take Away—A Favorite Verse to Carry With You

Consider buying a new Bible and reading one chapter a day. Each day underline your favorite verse from the chapter you read. After you are finished reading the entire book, go back and circle one verse that is your favorite verse of the book from the ones that you underlined in each chapter. Write a few sentences in your Bible about why that is your favorite verse for that book. After you've read the whole Bible, you'll have 1,189 favorite verses underlined (one from each chapter) and sixty-six all time favorite verses—one from each book. Think about how valuable that Bible will be to you, as you can now turn to any page in Scripture and remember which verse spoke to your heart the most. Then read your Bible a second time through and use a different color pen to repeat the process, but you aren't allowed to choose the same verses. Imagine how alive your Bible will become as you spend time in it over the years. It's a simple, but fruitful and personal way to study the Scriptures.

10. You Will Feel the Spiritual Battle

Satan will fight to keep you from meeting with the Lord each day. He hates nothing more than seeing a Christian getting down to business with God. He knows that such believers are dangerous to his kingdom of darkness, so watch for his tactics.

- The Battle of the Blankets: Almost every morning you will be tempted to hit the snooze button and sleep in and shorten or miss your quiet time with the Lord. Resist at all costs! Go to bed early enough and with thoughts of Scripture. Leave your Bible open to the passage you'll read the next morning, and get out of bed as soon as you wake up.

- Concentration: Our minds easily wander. So, be aware. If you are sleepy, pray aloud and with your eyes open in order to stay alert. Never have your quiet time in bed. Wake yourself up; take a shower, drink some coffee, eat breakfast. Remember to keep a notebook handy, so when your mind wanders to something you need to do that day, you can write it down and forget about it until later. Take control of wandering thoughts by constantly bringing your mind back with quiet firmness, and without scolding yourself.

- Dry Seasons: Sometimes you may feel like you are not getting anything out of your daily devotions. But obedience is more important than our emotions. Feelings come and go, but the Word of the Lord endures forever (1 Peter 1:25). If you only had your quiet time on the days when you felt like it, the Devil would make sure you never felt like it. Dry seasons come into all of our lives, some of the things that cause them are:

  - Disobedience—Are there sins that you need to confess?
  - Your physical condition—Are you getting enough rest?

- Rushing—Don't try to do too many things. Keep it simple.

- Routine—Watch for staleness—mix it up a little.

- Selfishness—Share your insights with others. Don't hog them!

Satan's strongest attacks will come in connection with your desire to be diligent in your quiet time. He knows that if he can keep you out of the Word, he has defeated you. If he can keep you from spending quality time with the Lord at the start of a day, then he's won the battle.

11. <u>Don't Give Up</u>

Wilbur Smith once said, "If the time has gone for our devotional reading on any one day before the chapter has yielded some truth for our souls, then we can give it further thought while riding down to work in your car or as you go about your normal activities…but do not let that particular passage in the Word remain for you a barren area: keep drilling through the soil and rock until you strike Living Water!"

If you miss a meal, it does not mean that you should give up eating. The same is true of your quiet time. It takes time to develop and maintain good habits. Remember, a habit is like a ball of twine: every time you drop it, many strands unwind. Develop good habits by doing your best to:

- <u>Be consistent</u>. By spending time with the Lord each day, you will develop a habit that will become rooted in your life.

- <u>Avoid exceptions</u>. Steer clear of anything that takes you away from your quiet time. Recognize that yielding to such distractions will only reinforce the idea that other things are more important.

Our daily devotions should be as regular as our mealtimes. Be aware of allowing too many exceptions to occur, even those you feel will be "just this once." One reason why I'm stressing this so much is because whether you are involved in ministry, or desiring to be a witness for the Lord in the workplace or on campus, or raising young children in your home, wherever the Lord has you, you will never be able to take another person any farther spiritually, than you have gone yourself. So a good question to ask is, "If everyone else had the same devotional time that I have—how would they be doing spiritually?"

BASIC BIBLE STUDY METHODS

Simple Ways for Everyone to Study God's Word

The following study methods are sure to bless every believer who wants to develop good study habits and grow in their love for and understanding of, God and His Word.

chapter

06

Daily Bread

The Lord sustained His people for forty years in the wilderness by miraculously providing fresh manna each morning. Regardless of how much manna they collected, it was always enough nourishment for that day. Similarly, the Lord wants to sustain us, every day, with fresh "spiritual manna" from His Word. The *Daily Bread* Bible study is one of the simplest ways to begin discovering the specific truths that the Holy Spirit has for us each day. This method involves five steps that will help you to meditate on a single passage of Scripture, discover its full meaning, and begin applying it to your life.

To begin your *Daily Bread* Bible study, follow these simple steps:

Step 1 Choose a passage, paragraph, or chapter to study

You will get the best results when you work your way through the Bible systematically rather than randomly. By studying the Scriptures in this way, you will also become familiar with the whole counsel of God's Word.

Step 2 Pray—Ask God to meet with you

Before you begin your Bible study, spend time in prayer asking the Lord to reveal Himself to you through His Word. Ask the Holy Spirit to help you see Jesus today.

Step 3 Think about the passage you are studying

Reread the passage a number of times and thoughtfully consider what it is saying. Meditate upon the meaning of the text and how you can apply it to your life. Apply these six "P's" as you think through the passage:

- Picture it! Visualize the scene. Imagine how you would react if you were there. How would you have felt to be a part of what was going on? Is there anything in your life today that you can compare this situation to?

- Pronounce it! Read the verse aloud several times placing emphasis on a different word each time. Note the different shade of meaning that is added by reading Psalm 25:15 in this way:

"**MY** eyes are ever toward the LORD..."
(This is personal—my responsibility.)

"My **EYES** are ever toward the LORD..."
(What are my eyes focused on today?)

"My eyes **ARE** ever toward the LORD..."
(Are, reveals a resolute position.)

"My eyes are **EVER** toward the LORD..."
(Forever and always: no turning away.)

"My eyes are ever **TOWARD** the LORD..."
(Am I heading toward Him today?)

"My eyes are ever toward **THE** LORD..."
(He is the one and only Lord!)

"My eyes are ever toward the **LORD**..."
(Make a list of the names and attributes of the Lord.)

- Paraphrase it! Restating the passage in your own words helps you to understand it better. Using contemporary language to express timeless biblical truths helps you to bridge the gap between the past and the present.

- Personalize it! Put your name in place of the nouns or pronouns that are used in the Scripture and read it aloud (i.e., For God so loved _____).

- <u>Pray it!</u> Make the verse a prayer. The best way to express faith in God is by taking the promises and truths found in His Word and praying them back to Him.

- <u>Probe it!</u> Use the **S-P-A-C-E-P-E-T-S** acrostic (refer to page 36) to help you locate the different themes of the passage.

Step 4 Plan one application

Write down one application based on the insights you have discovered through your study of the text. Writing your thoughts down will help you to fully think them through and make them easier to remember and apply. It has been proven that writing promotes memory, and helps you to express what you have learned more clearly, to others. Remember to make your application personal, practical, and provable.

Step 5 Carry your favorite verse with you

On a small piece of paper (i.e., post-it-note or index card) write down the verse that impacted you the most from your study and carry it with you throughout the day. Occasionally, pull the card out and read the verse. This will help you recall what you studied and keep those truths fresh in your thoughts. You might also want to use this system to begin memorizing Scripture.

The next page has a sample of the Daily Bread Bible study method.

DAILY BREAD

SCRIPTURE – matthew 6:22-23

PICTURE IT – Jesus is using the picture of a lamp to help illustrate how just as a lamp guides your way and gives you helpful light to navigate a path, so too when your eye is focused on Godly things, you won't stumble into sin. I'm picturing a traveler on a dark path with a lamp.

PRONOUNCE IT – helpful emphasis below
...your WHOLE body... – all of me, my thoughts
...your whole BODY... – my physical, human flesh can be directed by a spiritual use of my eyes
...will be FULL of light... – my flesh feels full of sinful thoughts at times, but this promise says my entire being can be full of godliness!

PARAPHRASE IT – The guide of my life is my eye. If my vision is focused on Godly things, then all of my being will be filled with God's Word. (Psalm 119:105)

PERSONALIZE IT – The lamp of Andy's body is his eye. Therefore, if Andy's eye is good, then his whole body will be full of light...

PRAY IT - Father, help my focus today to be good. I want to think about and look at only things that edify me (Philippians 4:8)

PROBE IT - using SPACE PETS acrostic
S - Letting my eyes look at darkness (ungodliness)
P - Focus my eye, and God focuses all of me!
A - Be serious about visual temptations.
C - Matthew 5:28 - sins of the eyes
E - Joseph - flee sin, don't look upon it
P - Lord, fix my bad eyes
E - Living in darkness by being distracted by world
T - God's Word is my light!
S - His forgiveness when I have a bad eye

PLAN APPLICATION - I'm going to start reviewing movies before I see them in the theater to see if they will be bad for my eyes.

PORTABLE VERSE - v.22
I'm memorizing this verse by the end of the week!

chapter
07

Timothy Method

A sk yourself this simple question: What purpose does the Bible serve? In 2 Timothy 3:16-17, we read: "All Scripture is given by inspiration of God, and is profitable for doctrine, for reproof, for correction, for instruction in righteousness, that the man of God may be complete, thoroughly equipped for every good work." These two verses give us the four main purposes that Scripture serves in the life of a believer. It is for:

1. Doctrine

2. Reproof

3. Correction

4. Instruction in righteousness

The *Timothy Method* examines the text in light of these four main purposes. Studying Scripture in this way will help you understand the purpose for which it was written. The Bible is always useful to "teach us what is true and to make us realize what is wrong in our lives. It straightens us out and teaches us to do what is right" (2 Timothy 3:16, NLT).

Follow these four steps to begin your *Timothy Method* Bible study:

Step 1 Doctrine (NKJV), Teaching (NIV)
Doctrine, or teaching, reveals what is right. As you study, ask yourself what doctrine or truth is being taught in the verse. Then break your answer down into a simple statement (i.e., this verse teaches about the authority

of Scripture). To help you to determine what the main teaching of the text is, ask as many questions as necessary. For example:

- Does this verse help me understand God's character?
- Does this verse help to clarify God's will for my life?
- Does this verse reveal a biblical truth?

Step 2 Reproof (NKJV), Rebuking (NIV)

Reproof, or rebuking, reveals what is wrong. God's standard is perfect and right. As you study and discover what the passage is teaching, ask yourself if you are obeying or resisting this truth in your life. You can determine this by answering these questions:

- Are there areas in my life where I'm not living out the teaching?
- If yes: note when, where, and how you are violating this truth.
- What are the consequences of not living by this truth?

Step 3 Correction (NKJV), Correcting (NIV)

Correction, or correcting, reveals how to get right. After the Holy Spirit convicts us of sin, the next thing we need to do is to repent. Repenting means doing a complete turn-around. If you are not sure how to do that, ask yourself:

- What would be the opposite of this sin?
- What do I need to do to start heading in the right direction?

Step 4 Instruction (NKJV), Training (NIV)

Instruction, or training in righteousness allows us to develop discipline in order to continue to live rightly. Once we know the truth, and have repented of our sin, we need to keep walking in that direction. What are some changes that you can make today that will help you to continually resist sin, and grow spiritually? Ask yourself these questions:

- What action can I take that will fortify my commitment and ensure I don't stumble in sin?
- How can I know if I am walking in the Spirit?

By slowing down and applying these four simple steps to your study of God's Word, you have hopefully: (1) Discovered (or been reminded of) a biblical truth, (2) considered whether you are living out this truth, (3) mapped out any corrective measures needed if you are not, and (4) came up with a plan to continue living righteously before the Lord.

The next page has a sample of the Timothy Method Bible study method.

TIMOTHY METHOD

SCRIPTURE - Ephesians 4:1-6

DOCTRINE - We have been called by God, and ought to walk worthy of that calling. One of the most important ways to walk worthy is to be in unity with other believers.

REPROOF - Though I know it's important, I don't always walk in unity with my brothers and sisters, usually for selfish reasons.

CORRECTION - Walking in unity is not always easy, but it is extremely important. I must work hard to 'keep the unity' of the Spirit.'

INSTRUCTION - Because walking in unity pleases my Father, I am going to seek His help. Whenever I find myself becoming angry with someone, I will stop what I am doing and pray that God will help me to see that we are one body and ought to walk in unity.

chapter
08

SPECS ON

M any people wear eyeglasses or contact lenses to help them see more clearly. Years ago eyeglasses were commonly called spectacles, or specs for short. To those who wear specs, everything seems blurry without them; but with them, all things come into focus. This devotional Bible study method, *SPECS ON*, works in much the same way as a pair of eyeglasses—it brings clarity to God's Word.

In Psalm 119:18, David wrote, "Open my eyes, that I may see wondrous things from Your law." We want to ask God to open our eyes and give us clarity and direction from His Word. We want Him to sharpen our focus so we can see the application He has for us. We will accomplish this by remembering the acronym, **SPECS ON**! So it's time to put your *SPECS ON*, and let's begin studying God's Word.

Follow these four simple steps to begin your *SPECS ON* Bible study:

Step 1 Select a chapter and read it three times
Read slowly, soaking in all the details of the passage. As you read, look for some practical insight on how to become more like Jesus.

Step 2 Ask yourself, what...
On a blank chart, write the acronym—SPECS ON—down the left hand side of the sheet, leaving room on the right for your findings. During this step we'll only deal with the SPECS part. Each time the Lord shows you something that matches one of these categories write it down in the appropriate space. You do not have to try to answer the questions in order.

You may not always be able to answer all of the questions—that's okay. The point is to slow down and think through what you are reading; developing an eye so you can see what God is making clear in His Word. Ask yourself, what...

S	- **Sin** I need to forsake
P	- **Promise** I need to claim
E	- **Example** I need to follow
C	- **Command** I need to obey
S	- **Stumbling** block I need to avoid
O	- **Obedience** Needed
N	- **New** Information Learned

Step 3 Obedience Needed (Apply the Scriptures)

- What will you do differently because of what you learned?
- Make a practical plan to become a "doer" of the Word.
- Spend time in prayer asking God for strength to obey.

Step 4 New Information Learned

Review all of your answers and meditate on everything that God is showing you as you study His Scriptures:

- Did you learn anything new about God?
- Did you learn anything new about yourself?
- Thank God in prayer for these new truths.

It's amazing what God will show you when you put your *SPECS ON*.

The next page has a sample of the SPECS ON Bible study method.

S.P.E.C.S. QUESTIONS

SCRIPTURE - James 1

SINS TO FORSAKE - (v.26) I must learn to control my tongue and not say things that will displease God and hurt my brothers and sisters.

PROMISES TO CLAIM - (v.12) sometimes my life can be difficult, if I endure I will receive the crown of life.

EXAMPLES TO FOLLOW - (v.25) I want to follow the example of the person who looks into God's Word, and then makes the proper application to his life.

COMMANDS TO OBEY - (v.2) Count it all joy when I fall into various trials. (v.19) Be swift to hear, slow to speak, slow to wrath. (v.21) Lay aside all filthiness.

STUMBLING BLOCKS TO AVOID - (v.26-27) If I simply say that I am religious, but my life doesn't reflect it. I have deceived myself and my religion is useless. I must not only say, but I must also do!

OBEY - MY APPLICATION - (v.27) God cares about widows and orphans and I will seek to be a blessing to them also. Right now, I will google the nearest orphanage and call them to see if they allow visitors.

NEW INSIGHTS - True religion is such that it manifests itself in the life of a person in not only what they say, but how they live. I have learned from this passage that religion that pleases God is that which will manifest itself in holy living.

chapter
09

Rethink and Restate

Christians love to experience God's Word personally. One way we can do that is by paraphrasing the Scripture that we are studying. Restating the text in our own words helps us to digest it and forces us to think about what it is saying as we attempt to reword it. The purpose of this exercise is not to alter the meaning, but to *Rethink and Restate* the passage.

Three Different Types of Paraphrases

1. A normal paraphrase: Take the passage one phrase at a time and reword it. Change the entire phrase, leaving no word untouched.

2. A compact paraphrase: Reduce the passage to two-thirds, one-half, or even one-third of its original length. Find the core message, and don't leave any of the essential parts out.

3. An extended paraphrase: Expand the passage to as much as twice its original length by explaining the meaning of the passage by inserting brief commentaries [in brackets] as you read the verses.

Here are step-by-step instructions that will help you paraphrase Scripture:

Step 1 Select a short passage (approximately three verses)

Choose a verse that is meaningful to you, one that has comforted you in the past or helped you through a personal struggle.

Step 2 Read the passage slowly and repeatedly (five times)

- Pay attention to any natural breaks in words and phrases.

- Write the verse one word or phrase per line; skip three lines to allow room for your paraphrase underneath.

Step 3 Pause to pray

- Ask God to help you understand and restate His Word accurately.

- Pray that you will know and experience His presence more intimately through His Word.

Step 4 Rewrite each phrase using your own words

- Personalize the verse. Wherever you read the words, "you" or "we" substitute your name or "me."

- If any words in the text relate to your current circumstances restate the passage using your particular situation.

- Use appropriate synonyms and have a thesaurus handy to help you find the best words to use as substitutes.

Variation: Be Creative as You Paraphrase

1. Restate every illustration using a modern example. For instance, instead of saying the Word of God is "sharper than any two-edged sword" you might say it is "sharper than a surgeon's scalpel."

2. Imagine that you are writing these words in a letter format to someone very close to you, who is a new believer (i.e., a friend or family member), and attempt to explain these truths in a way that they would understand

---

Step 5 Read your paraphrase and meditate on its truth

Take time to think about the Scripture you paraphrased. Is the meaning clearer to you now than it was before?

Step 6 Application—Become a doer of His Word

Plan to obey God's Word today.

The next page has a sample of the Rethink and Restate Bible study method.

RETHINK + RESTATE

SCRIPTURE - John 3:16

TYPE OF PARAPHRASE - Extended

For God - My loving Father in heaven
so loved - so very deeply cherished
the world - everyone on the whole planet
that He gave - that He offered sacrificially
His only begotten Son - the greatest and most
                needed gift, His precious Child
that whoever - that no matter who you are or
                what you've done
believes - if you just have simple faith
in Him - in Jesus Christ your Savior,
should not perish - you won't die and go to hell,
but have - instead you'll posess an
everlasting - unending and eternal
life - perfect and joyful life in heaven.

APPLICATION - When I paraphrase this
familiar verse, it causes me to rejoice in the
depth and height of God's love for me. I am
going to spend time in prayer thanking God
for this love and asking Him how I can be
more loving to others myself.

chapter

10

Alphabet Method

A nother study method that will help you to slow down and think about God's Word in a practical and personal way is the *Alphabet Method*. It is as easy as, A B C D E F.

God created language and authored the Bible in order to communicate with us. We can be certain that when we sit down and desire to hear from Him in His Word, He also desires to speak to us. The *Alphabet Method* of Bible study is one way to record what God is saying as we spend time in the Scriptures.

You may want to modify this method by adding more letters to the acronym, or personalizing it to suite your style and personality. The main thing is to remember to enjoy God's Word.

Follow these seven steps to begin your *Alphabet Method* Bible study:

Step 1 Choose a passage of Scripture and read it

Prayerfully read the chosen passage at least three times. Read it differently each time: first read it silently, then aloud, and finally pausing for a time of reflection at the end of each verse.

Step 2 A = A title

The title you choose should be one that clearly identifies the main theme of the passage and is memorable (make it fun). You will probably want to do this after you have become more familiar with the content.

Step 3 B = Best verse

The best verse is the one that you like the most out of the passage you just read. Write down that verse reference.

Step 4 C = Cross-reference

How does the rest of the Bible shed light on these verses? Find cross-references for every verse. Chart these references and include space for a brief description summarizing each passage. Afterwards, refer back to all of the summaries. How do these verses, together, enhance your understanding of God's Word?

Step 5 D = Difficulties

Read each verse. Are any of them too difficult for you to explain to someone else? If so, write down the verse reference and the question you have about its meaning—be specific. Now, do your own study, checking the context, similar passages, commentaries, and so forth, until you are able to answer your own questions. If you are still stumped after doing your own study discuss your questions with other mature believers, and refer to commentaries. Don't stop until you are satisfied that your questions are all answered. Now you are ready to share your insights with others.

Step 6 E = Essentials

Outline or summarize the most important points of the passage. In this step, you are only observing and recording what the passage says, not what it means. An outline divides the passage into its natural paragraphs, giving a brief title or heading to each section. List as many sub-points under each of the main headings as needed to define the contents. A summary is simply a retelling of the main subject of the passage.

Step 7 F = Final thoughts

As you have been slowly reading and studying God's Word, what have you been able to take away from your time? What do you feel God has been speaking to you? Is any change required in your life? What is your personal application today?

The next page has a sample of the Alphabet Method Bible study.

ALPHABET METHOD

SCRIPTURE – Hebrews 11:13-16

A — A TITLE - Our Heavenly Hope

B — BEST VERSE – v. 16

C — CROSS REFERENCES

v.	cross ref.	summary
13	1 Peter 2:11	As a pilgrim, I should stay away from sin
14	Hebrews 13:14	Our homeland is not found here.
15	Isaiah 43:18-19	We must forget the old and press towards the new
16	John 14:2	He has prepared a home for us

D — DIFFICULTIES – (v.13) In what way were those pilgrims assured of those promises?

E — ESSENTIALS - As a Christian, I'm like a pilgrim on my way home. I am to trust God and walk by faith, realizing heaven is my home.

F — FINAL THOUGHTS - From this text, I am reminded how important it is to have a heavenly attitude in all my earthly activities.

chapter

11

One at a Time

Most of us have a special verse or two of Scripture, and regardless of how often we read them they continue to speak powerfully to us. This Bible study method is geared toward helping us dig even deeper into those all-time favorite life verses, in order to pull out every pearl of wisdom. The Word of God is alive, that is why even one Scripture can captivate our hearts and instruct us in so many different ways. If you are tempted to pass on this method because you think you already know everything about your favorite verses, think again. The Bible is always worth rereading, and those special verses where the Lord speaks so personally to us, are the ones we should reread often. Why not let God surprise you one more time?

Hebrews 4:12 says, "the word of God is living and powerful, and sharper than any two-edged sword, piercing even to the division of soul and spirit, and of joints and marrow, and is a discerner of the thoughts and intents of the heart." His Word will speak to you right where you are today, just like in times past.

Follow these simple instructions to begin a *One at a Time* Bible study:

Step 1 Write out the verse you are studying

Read the verse repeatedly—seven to ten times—and then write it out in its entirety. Writing out a verse helps us remember it.

Step 2 Rewrite the verse in your own words

Write out the verse again using your own words this time. What is the central theme? Does the verse contain a commandment, a promise, a warning, a doctrine?

Step 3 Think about possible meanings

Write down all the possible meanings of this verse that you can think of (at least three). What was the writer's intended meaning? Now, choose the most likely meaning.

Step 4 Think about questions you have

Write any questions you have about this verse. Would your friends or family have any difficulty with any part of this verse?

Step 5 Check the context

For a better understanding, read the verse in context. Read the verses immediately before your verse, and write down how they add to your understanding of the passage you are studying. Now read the verses directly after your verse, and write down any additional insights you get from reading them. How is the picture clearer with this information? Where is the writer going with his thought? Context is necessary for a complete understanding of a passage.

Step 6 Decide on your application

Now that you have spent time observing the verse, how do you think God wants you to respond? Write out any thoughts and impressions you have concerning how you could begin applying this verse to your life. Become a doer of the Word! Remember, it is important to give yourself a deadline or else you may never do anything. Start today!

The next page has a sample of the One at a Time Bible study method.

ONE AT A TIME

SCRIPTURE - 1 Timothy 1:12
"And I thank Christ Jesus our Lord who has enabled me, because He counted me faithful, putting me into the ministry.

MESSAGE - Paul is so very grateful that Christ chose and equipped him and put him into the ministry, serving the Lord by serving His people.

POSSIBLE MEANINGS - "He counted me faithful"- what does this part mean?
· because of Paul's past life of faithfulness
· because God knew Paul would do a great job once God did call him to ministry.
· because God saw him as perfect in Jesus

CONTEXT - (v.11) It was the gospel that was committed to Paul's trust. Thus as Paul is engaged in ministry, it's the gospel he is to communicate

(v.13) We see why Paul is so thankful to the Lord as Paul mentions what he was like before he was born again.

QUESTIONS - How did God call Paul faithful when you look at what he says of himself in v.13?

APPLICATION - Despite my "pre-Jesus" life, God counted me faithful and has called me to serve Him. I'm going to prayerfully examine my heart for a weakness that could cause me to be unfaithful to God, and I'll memorize a verse that can help me when I'm tempted in that weakness.

chapter

12

Six Searches

With this method all you need to do is read a passage of Scripture—it can be one paragraph, one chapter, or even one of the smaller books. Read it prayerfully and thoughtfully, slowing down whenever it is necessary, in order for you to fully grasp what the writer intended to convey. Now, simply follow this six-point plan that will help you ask the right questions, and get the most out of every passage of Scripture.

To complete a *Six Searches* Bible study, simply ask yourself:

Step 1 What did you like?

Was there something exciting that God showed you? Write a few sentences about why you liked that particular part of the passage.

Step 2 What didn't you like?

Be honest, was there anything you didn't like? Maybe you thought it was boring, or maybe you disagreed with what is being said. It is okay to let the Lord know your thoughts; after all, He already knows them. But, as you express your thoughts, ask Him to help you change your mind where you need to come into agreement with His Word. Write down your thoughts in a few sentences.

Step 3 What didn't you understand?

Did anything confuse you? Do you have any questions about what you read? Every time we read the Bible it becomes clearer to us, but occasionally questions arise that need answers. Where can we find those answers?

Begin by writing down your questions, concerns, and any topics you'd like to further explore. When you have more time, start to dig a little deeper to find the answers.

Step 4 What did you learn about God?

The Bible teaches us about God, so write down everything you learn about Him. Sum up your thoughts in a short paragraph.

Step 5 What should you do?

In the Scriptures God gives us commands, guidelines, recommendations, advice, and examples. From this, we choose whether we are going to follow Him. Did God show you anything specific in your study that you need to obey? Write down those things and make a decision to follow God's instruction to you today.

Step 6 What phrase can you take with you today?

Reread the passage. What stands out to you as the most important phrase? What are the keywords? Choose one phrase or verse that sums up the main lesson that God taught you from the passage. Write it down on a piece of paper and carry it with you. Throughout the day, take it out and reflect on the time you spent with God in His Word.

The next page has a sample of the Six Searches Bible study method.

SIX SEARCHES

[SCRIPTURE] – James 1

[I LIKED] – (v. 17) This verse shows me that God really loves me to give me such good gifts.

[I DIDN'T LIKE] – (v. 2) This verse shows me how selfish my heart is. If it were up to me, God I would not have any trials! But if I must have them, I'm glad there is hope.

[I DIDN'T UNDERSTAND] – (v. 27) How do I keep myself "unspotted from the world"? What does that mean? Should I hide?

[I LEARNED] – (v. 26-27) What true religion really is in God's eyes. Wow, was I off! God's priorities for religion make it really practical day by day and not just about going to church.

[I SHOULD] – (v. 4) Let patience grow me as a Christian. I can be very impatient.

[I'LL TAKE WITH ME] – (v. 3-4) I'm writing these verses on notecards and I'm going to keep them in my wallet for a week until I memorize them.

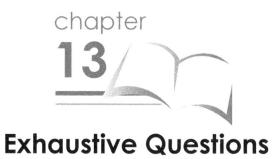

chapter 13

Exhaustive Questions

We often read the Bible too quickly. We tend to skip over the difficult parts in order to get to the parts that we like. It feels good to read those passages that we love and enjoy, but we are actually missing out on discovering some great truths when we read the Bible this way. Those who desire to find treasure must dig for it as a miner digs for the hidden gems beneath the earth's surface. A half-hearted, indifferent attitude towards God's Word will not yield very much. It's only when you roll up your sleeves and get to work that you will discover the richness buried within the pages of Scripture. Proverbs 25:2 says, "It is the glory of God to conceal a matter, but the glory of kings is to search out a matter."

The Holy Spirit is the One who authored the Scriptures and He is available to reveal their riches to us; all we have to do is ask Him. Learning to ask questions, as you spend time with the Lord in your Bible study, will help you discover details you would have otherwise missed. Be determined to interview the text; have the mind of a reporter. Interrogate the Scriptures by asking anything that comes to mind—any question you'd like answered. Be exhaustive and more likely you'll be successful!

Follow these simple steps to do an *Exhaustive Questions* Bible study:

Step 1 Choose a chapter of the Bible and read it three times
Read slowly, making note of anything that doesn't make sense.

Step 2 Write down three or more questions for each verse

Yes, that is a lot, but that is the point of the *Exhaustive Questions* study method. You are to ask about everything. Refer to the questions found on pages 24 and 25 as a guide.

Step 3 Research five questions from the entire chapter

Pick these five questions from the ones you have already written down. What are you most curious about? Does the passage contain any words or phrases that you don't understand? Does it mention people or places that you never heard of before? Ask anything and everything.

Step 4 Find the answers!

Never leave a good question unanswered. It may take time and you may need to utilize a concordance, cross-references, commentaries, Bible handbook, online Bible resources, and even your pastor, to help you come to the correct interpretation of the text. But do whatever it takes to understand the truth.

Step 5 Apply the answer

What is one personal application that you can make from the Scriptures you studied?

Step 6 Tell someone

Choose the answer to the one question that impacted you most, and share your discovery with someone else. Ask them questions as if it were a Bible trivia game.

The next page has a sample of the Exhaustive Questions Bible study.

EXHAUSTIVE QUESTIONS

SCRIPTURE - Psalm 126

QUESTIONS

v.1: Q1. What does captivity mean?
    Q2. Where is Zion?
    Q3. Is this a real event or only a dream?

v.2: Q1. Who is the 'our' referring to?
    Q2. What nations?
    Q3. Why did they laugh and sing?

v.3: Q1. What were the great things God did?
    Q2. Is "us" Israel or Judah or all believers?
    Q3. Did they deserve it?

v.4: Q1. I still don't know what captivity means?
    Q2. Why would they "want" captivity?
    Q3. What are streams in the south?

v.5: Q1. What does sow mean?
    Q2. What is being sown?
    Q3. What does reap mean?

v.6: Q1. Is it good to weep a lot?
    Q2. What is a sheave?
    Q3. I don't farm. How do I bear seed for
       sowing?

ANSWERS -

v.1: Q2 - Zion is a mountain in Jerusalem. Since Jerusalem is the capital of Israel, Zion began to refer to that area of land and the people who dwelt there.

v.2: Q2 - The nations were the gentile peoples who surrounded the nation of Israel.

v.3: Q1 - The great thing God did was to free them from their captivity and slavery.

v.4: Q3 - The streams in the south were rivers that would normally dry up in the dry seasons.

v.6: Q2 - A sheave is a bundle of grain.

APPLY - Just as it was a great thing for these people to be delivered from their captivity, so also it is a great thing that I have been delivered from sin and Satan. Like them, I will sing of my salvation.

chapter

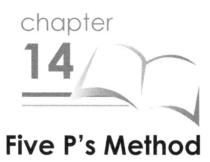

14

Five P's Method

Daily Bible study is essential because we need God's wisdom in order to meet each day's challenges. The *Five P's Method* is a great way to apply Scriptural truths to our daily circumstances. This method helps us to recognize the timeless principles found in Scripture, and relate them to our lives.

Follow these steps to begin your *Five P's Method* Bible study:

On a blank piece of paper, make five columns with the following headings:

- Principle of Conduct
- Put Another Way
- Personal Struggle
- Profit or Loss Anticipated
- Plan of Action

Step 1 Principle of conduct

In the first column, write one verse from your daily reading that states a life principle.

Step 2 Put another way

In this column, briefly explain and restate the verse in your own words.

Step 3 Personal struggle

How is this principle connected to the problems/challenges you personally face today? Write down key areas where you can begin to apply it in your own life.

Step 4 Profit or Loss Anticipated

It is always wise to consider the benefits of following God, versus the cost of not following Him. In this column, list all the blessings that you can think of that will come from obedience to this principle. Also, list all the possible consequences of disobedience. Be exhaustive. The more you think about the value of following God's guidelines, the better motivated you will be to act upon them.

Step 5 Plan of action

When it comes to obeying God's Word, it's not the thought that counts. Good intentions are great, but only as we begin applying the Scriptures to our lives will we begin to be changed by them. Use this column to develop your own personal plan of action. Set deadlines for yourself, and if you need accountability, ask someone else to help you to stick to your plan.

The next page has a sample of the Five P's Method of Bible study.

5 P'S METHOD

SCRIPTURE - Matthew 6:33

PRINCIPLE OF CONDUCT	PUT IT ANOTHER WAY	PERSONAL STRUGGLE
"But seek first the kingdom of God and His righteousness and all these things shall be added unto you"	My main priority in life ought not to be the acquiring and accumulating of material possesions, but rather seeking out God's eternal kingdom.	There is always a temptation to make the pursuit of my life to gain worldly goods. The problem is, these material goods never satisfy, they only create a desire for more. Seeking first God's kingdom frees me from this.

PROFIT OR LOSS I CAN LOOK FORWARD TO	PLAN MY ACTION
God has promised to provide for all of my needs. Thus if I choose to make seeking His kingdom my ultimate priority, I can rest in the reality that He will provide for me. If I choose to disobey and make pursuing worldly gain my main priority, I can be sure that discouragement and disappointment await me.	Throughout the course of this next week, I am going to begin my day by writing down a list of things I will do that day, and next to that, a note or two about how I can seek God in each event.

MAJOR BIBLE STUDY METHODS

Time-tested Approaches for Those
Who Want to Go Deeper

The following time-tested techniques are designed to encourage every Christian to "major" in God's Word. They are meant to help believers grow beyond the basics, discover the richness of the Scriptures, and become familiar with its central themes, key topics, and main message. Most importantly, each of these study methods will encourage you to become a "doer" of God's Word. Applying the lessons will literally change the way you live.

chapter

15

Verse-by-Verse Charting

The *Verse-by-Verse Charting* method helps you to slow down and meditate on a few verses each day. No matter how many times you read a particular passage, the Holy Spirit can still teach you more about its meaning. This method of Bible study uses a five-column chart (see the example at the end of the chapter).

To begin a *Verse-by-Verse Charting* study, follow these instructions:

Step 1 Choose the verses

Select five to ten verses that you would like to study. If you'd like to study a chapter, you can use this method over the course of a few days.

Step 2 Write the verses out

In the first column, write out the verses you are studying in their entirety.

Step 3 Prepare a paraphrase

In the second column, write your own paraphrase of the verses. Be careful not to add your opinions—just stick to the facts, and try to reduce the word count rather than expand it. If you aren't sure of how to paraphrase the verses, then read another translation and write that down instead.

Step 4 Questions and answers

In column three, write any questions you have on the meaning of the passage, specific words, expressions, people, or ideas. Then do some research and write down as many answers as you are able to find to your questions.

Step 5 Find cross-references

Find at least one cross-reference for every verse. You can use a study Bible or concordance to help you find appropriate cross-references. List them in the fourth column.

Step 6 Meditate on each verse

When complete, review columns one to four and pray that God would help you come to a deeper understanding of His Word. As you meditate on the verses, briefly summarize your insights. If you are still uncertain about anything in the passage, check a commentary for additional help.

Another way to meditate on the verse is to take out all the verbs and arrange them in order. For example, Romans 8:28 says, "And we know that all things work together for good to those who love God, to those who are the called according to His purpose." The four verbs are: know, work together, love, and are. Looking at these action words helps us realize what our conduct should be as we attempt to live this truth out.

Step 7 Application (below your chart)

Finally, if any specific personal application comes to mind as you are studying, make note of it below the chart. Remember to set a deadline on taking action, and ask someone to hold you accountable if necessary so that you will be a doer of the Word. Note: If you haven't found an application, your time in the Word is not finished. Every good study ends in understanding how God wants you to respond to His Word.

The next page has a sample of the Verse-by-Verse Bible study method.

VERSE BY VERSE CHARTING

SCRIPTURE – 1 Timothy 4:12-14

VERSE	PARAPHRASE
v. 12 – "Let no man despise your youth, but be an example to the believers in word, in conduct, in love, in spirit, in faith, in purity."	Don't let anyone look down on you for your age...
v. 13 – "Till I come, give attention to reading, to exhortation, to doctrine."	Till I get there focus on reading, comforting, teaching
v. 14 – "Do not neglect the gift that is in you by prophecy with the laying on of the hands of the eldership.	Don't waste the gift you were given when the elders laid hands on you.

Q + A	CROSS REF.	MEDITATION
Q. How old was Timothy? A. We are not quite sure, but most likely younger than 30.	Titus 2:15 Philippians 3:17	No matter what my age, God can use me if I'm willing to live His way.
Q. What is doctrine? A. Core teachings that make up what you believe	2 Timothy 4:2	Knowing doctrine is essential for my life as a Christian.
Q. What does "laying on of the hands" mean? A. Simply when an elder prays for you.	2 Timothy 1:6 Acts 6:6	What gifts has God given me? I must not neglect them, but stir them up for His glory.

APPLICATION

My ministry will be significantly more effective if it is simply anchored on the Word of God. I will begin a Bible study on the core doctrines of the Christian faith by the end of this week.

chapter

16

Chapter Overview

The *Chapter Overview* method of Bible study involves, reading one chapter of Scripture a number of times, asking a few thought provoking questions, and then summarizing the main idea of the passage. It will take between one and two hours to study a chapter this way, but once you have you will own it, like never before. This method will breathe new life into your favorite chapters and help you come to a better understanding of those chapters that have confused you in the past. As Wilbur M. Smith once wrote, "It is one thing to read a chapter of the Bible: it is another thing to get something out of it for your own soul."

Follow these instructions to do a *Chapter Overview* Bible study:

Step 1 Read the chapter three times

Here are some hints on how to read a chapter of the Bible:

- Read it once, silently, in the translation you normally use. (*Don't stop to take notes, just look for the main idea, and try to follow the flow of thought.*)

- Read it again in a different translation. (*I like to use a contemporary translation for this second reading, usually the Amplified Bible, New Living Translation, or New International Version.*)

- Read it one last time, aloud, in the translation you normally use. (*Reading it aloud will help you to concentrate better and keep your mind from wandering.*)

Step 2 Follow these ten "C" instructions

1. What would you <u>CALL</u> this chapter?

   Give the chapter a title. Be descriptive and creative.

2. <u>COMPACT</u> the story.

   Summarize, outline, or paraphrase the entire chapter.

3. What is <u>CRYPTIC</u> about the chapter?

   What questions or problems do you have with understanding the meaning? Can you find answers?

4. Find <u>CROSS-REFERENCES</u>.

   What other passages in the Bible help you to understand this chapter?

5. Identify <u>CONSIDERABLE</u> people.

   Who are the notable characters in the chapter? Why are they included? What is significant about them?

6. Recognize <u>COMPELLING</u> words.

   Do you notice any key or repeated words or phrases?

7. Write the <u>CRITICAL</u> verse.

   What is your favorite verse and why do you like it so much?

8. Look for <u>CHRIST</u> in the passage.

   Is Jesus mentioned in the chapter? If not, does anything in the text remind you of Him? Look carefully—He is there!

9. What is the <u>CENTRAL</u> lesson?

   What is the main point of this chapter? What idea weaves it together?

10. <u>CREATE</u> an application.

    What has God shown you in this chapter? What is your response to the knowledge you have gained?

Answering these ten "C" questions provides a broad overview of the chapter that you are studying in the Bible.

The next page has a sample of the Chapter Overview Bible study method.

CHAPTER OVERVIEW

SCRIPTURE - 2 Samuel 9

CALL IT - The Kindness of God

COMPACT THE STORY
- David looking for someone to bless (v.1-3)
- David seeks out Mephibosheth (v.4-5)
- David and Mephibosheth meet (v.6-7)
- Mephibosheth responds humbly (v.8)
- David commands Ziba to bless Mephibosheth (v.9-10)
- Ziba agrees (v.11)
- David treats Mephibosheth like a son (v.11)
- Mephibosheth's family described (v.12-13)

WHAT IS CRYPTIC? - (v.8-9)
Why doesn't David answer his question?

CROSS REFERENCES
- v.1 - 1 Samuel 20:15 - fulfills covenant...
- v.11 - 2 Samuel 16:1-4 - Ziba is shady...
- v.13 - 2 Samuel 19:24-30 - Mephibosheth is loyal...

CONSIDERABLE PEOPLE
- David - king of Israel
- Ziba - servant of the house of Saul
- Mephibosheth - a son of Jonathan
- Micha - Mephibosheth's son

COMPELLING WORDS - kindness, lame, table

CRITICAL VERSE - (v.3)
"whom I may show the kindness of God..."

CHRIST SIGHTINGS - (v.13)
Fellowship at the King's table (Matthew 26:29)

CENTRAL LESSON - (v.3)
Seek out people to show the "kindness of God."

CREATE AN APPLICATION
I need to prayerfully ask God who He wants me
to bless and then make a serious effort in
making that happen (v.3). They don't need to
deserve this kindness (v.8).

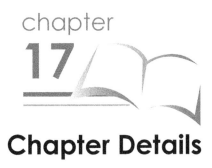

chapter

17

Chapter Details

A *Chapter Details* Bible study provides a better understanding of the chapter by carefully looking at the details of each paragraph, sentence, and word. The chart (see sample at the end of this chapter) works best on legal-sized paper.

Follow these steps to begin a *Chapter Details* Bible study:

Step 1 Write a summary of the chapter

Begin by reading the chapter three times. Do not try to interpret what you are reading at this time; just observe the facts, then summarize the chapter in one of the following two ways:

- Paraphrase it: Reword the chapter.

- Outline it: Create an outline following the paragraph divisions within the chapter. Give each paragraph a title, and list the sub-points beneath each title.

Step 2 Write your observations for each verse

In this step you are looking at every sentence and word and writing down everything you see. As you read, ask yourself: What does it say? (For more information on observing the text, review chapter two.)

Step 3 Write the interpretation for each verse

This step involves asking questions about the meaning of each verse, and finding the answers to those questions. As you read, ask the simple question: What does it mean? In this step, you will discover the main idea that the biblical writer intended to express. (For more on interpreting Scripture, review chapter three.)

Step 4 Find cross-references for each verse

Locating related Scriptures will help amplify the meaning of the passage being studied. You can often interpret passages that are not clear by reading similar passages that are clear. As you read, ask yourself: How do other Scriptures relate to and explain this one? You can find cross-references in the margins of your Bible.

There are a few different types of cross-references, including:

- The parallel cross-reference: It has almost exactly the same idea or wording as your verse.

- The story cross-reference: Narratives elsewhere in the Bible that illustrate the truth of what the verse is stating.

- The contrasting cross-reference: Sometimes approaching a subject from a contrasting viewpoint can help. For instance, it can be useful to see the consequences of someone who followed the opposite advice of the verse you are studying.

Step 5 List some possible applications for each verse

In this step, write down some possible applications. As you read, ask yourself: What will I do about what I have learned? Later, in step 7, you will choose one of these applications to work on for a week. (For more on application, review chapter four.)

Step 6 Write down some final thoughts on the chapter

Review your chart carefully and write down any final thoughts, insights, or conclusions that God has shown you regarding the chapter. Of all you have learned, what new truth excites you the most?

Step 7 Choose one application

From the list of possible applications that you made (see step 5), choose one and pray about a plan to do it!

The next page has a sample of the Chapter Details Bible study method.

CHAPTER DETAILS

SCRIPTURE - Genesis 23

SUMMARY
Sarah's Death and Burial
I. Sarah dies (v.1-2)
II. Abraham buys a grave and buries
 Sarah (v.3-20)
   A. Abraham's request (v. 3-9)
   B. Ephron's response (v.10-16)
   C. Abraham receives (v. 17-20)

OBSERVATIONS	INTERPRETATION
v.2-Sarah, Abraham's wife has passed away and Abraham mourns	There is no sorrow like that of death
v.7-Abraham is a stranger in the land, meeting with the sons of Heth	As a man of faith, Abraham was a pilgrim, just passing through

This is an example of the way the chart should look. A full study would be much more comprehensive and include the whole chapter in the chart.

↓

CROSS REF.	APPLICATIONS
John 11:35	My grandma doesn't have a relationship with God, and I don't know how much time she has. I'm going to pray about sharing Jesus with her next Thanksgiving.
Hebrews 11:13-16	I need to invest in my real home, heaven. I'm going to fill out a ministry application to serve at my church.

CONCLUDING THOUGHTS — Abraham is an example of a pilgrim, someone who walks by faith, knowing this world is not his home. In life, there will be pain, but we must keep our eyes on Jesus and He'll see us through.

chapter

18

Book Overview

An overview of the entire book helps you understand its basic structure. The word "section" on the chart represents either chapters or paragraphs depending on the size of the book being studied. If it is a lengthy book, the chart should be prepared using chapter divisions, however, if it is a shorter book it is better to break it down by paragraphs. Preparing this type of chart gives you a survey of the book's whole content and helps you see how the main theme is developed throughout.

Complete the following steps to start your *Book Overview* Bible study:

Step 1 Choose a book to study and read it

Write the book name at the top of the chart (see the example).

Step 2 Title each section

To determine the best title, ask yourself these two questions: What is the basic topic of this section? What is it saying about that topic? For example: if the basic topic is "obedience," your answer to the second question might be: "obedience is a solid foundation." Try to avoid making the title too general or too short. Remember, the title is meant to remind you of the specific topic of that section.

Step 3 Find and title the main divisions

Examine the title of each of the sections and relate them to the surrounding sections. To determine the main divisions of the book ask yourself: What do these sections have in common? The main divisions will overlap groups of section divisions, and should be entered vertically on the chart. Main divisions can occur between chapters and often are marked by changes in time, characters, themes, topics, or geographic locations.

Several different types of main divisions can occur on one chart. The book of Acts is a good illustration of the many ways the text can be divided.

We can divide Acts by its main characters:

- Ministry of Peter (chapters 1-12)
- Ministry of Paul (chapters 13-28)

We can divide Acts by its geographic location:

- Witness to Jerusalem (chapters 1-7)
- Witness to Judea and Samaria (chapters 8-12)
- Witness to the uttermost parts (chapters 13-28)

We can divide Acts based on what was happening in the church:

- The church established (chapters 1-7)
- The church scattered (chapters 8-12)
- The church extended (chapters 13-28)

We can divide Acts based on the group being ministered to:

- To the Jews (chapters 1-7)
- A transitional period (chapters 8-12)
- To the gentiles (chapters 13-28)

Step 4 Find the main theme of the book

Once you have determined the main divisions, you will begin to see the overall theme of the book more clearly. This is done simply by comparing the titles of each of the main divisions and asking these questions:

- What do they have in common?
- As a whole, what are they saying?

Do your best to define the overall message of the book in one sentence. This sentence is then entered on your chart, vertically along the left side of the main divisions to remind you that this theme runs throughout the book.

The next page has a sample of the Book Overview Bible study method.

BOOK OVERVIEW

[SCRIPTURE] - Romans

THEME: God's plan to redeem all hopeless men for holy living.

Man's Problem- Sin	1- Man is completely guilty
	2- Both Jew and Gentile guilty
	3- All have sinned
God's Solution- Faith in Christ (Gospel)	4- God is looking for faith
	5- Christ is our substitute
	6- We are dead to sin
	7- We are dead to the law
	8- We have life in Christ
God's Heart- Gospel To All People	9- Israel's rejection of gospel
	10- Israel's need for gospel
	11- Church's responsibility to Israel
Man's Response- Holy Living	12- Living as a Christian
	13- Obeying authority
	14- Love better than liberty
	15- Walking as a body
	16- Final greetings

chapter

19

Book Details

This method helps you to get into the details of any book of the Bible from a bird's-eye perspective. After reading the entire book several times without stopping you will then ask and answer a series of questions that will help you to draw a horizontal chart of the book's contents and gain a general understanding of the writer's purpose, theme, structure, and main message. Although the Bible is a compilation of sixty-six separate books, they each have a unique and important message for today. The *Book Details* method is a practical way to grasp the general contents of any single book of the Bible.

The following steps will help you to complete a *Book Details* Bible study:

Step 1 Prayerfully read the book

Read the book in its entirety and follow these suggestions:

- <u>Read the book in one sitting</u>. We suffer much from our fragmented reading of the Scriptures. Most books of the Bible are not too long to read in one sitting. However, for those that are, begin by reading all the paragraph titles along with the first sentence of each section. This will enable you to sense the general tone of the book from beginning to end. You will get a good idea of how it flows and where it is going.

- <u>Ignore the chapter divisions</u>. To get the main theme, read quickly and without stopping at chapter divisions.

- <u>Reread the book</u>. Read the book as many times as possible—the more you read it the better you will understand it.

Step 2 Take notes on what you are reading

In a notebook, write any impressions and/or important facts you discover in your reading. Explain how these passages aid your understanding of the text and enable you to see the book's bigger picture. (For more on the skill of observation, review chapter two.)

Ask questions like these and any other similar ones that might help:

- What is my <u>first impression</u> of this book?
- What <u>literary style</u> does the writer employ in this book?
- What are the key <u>repeated</u> words?
- Does the writer use <u>figurative speech</u> or a <u>logical argument</u> to make the main points?
- What is the <u>emotional tone</u> of the writer? ...of the hearers?
- How does what you are reading <u>make you feel</u>?

Step 3 Perform a background study of the book

Research the historical and geographical setting of the book. Many of the answers will be found in the text, so begin taking notice of the times and places that are mentioned. When you are finished reading, if you still have more questions than answers search other references such as, a study Bible, Bible dictionary, Bible encyclopedia, Bible handbook, or Bible atlas. However, discipline yourself to use these only after you have done your own personal research—discovering these truths in the text for yourself will make them yours for life.

Ask questions to learn more about the background of the book. Here are some examples:

- What can I learn about the <u>writer</u>?
- <u>Why, when, where, and to whom</u> was the book written?
- What <u>other background information</u> sheds light on this book?
- Where does this book fall <u>chronologically</u> within the Bible?
- What <u>geographic locations</u> are mentioned in this book?

Step 4 Make a detailed chart of the book's divisions

Create a diagramed layout of the book on a separate sheet of paper. This will help you to visualize the book's structure and content through its chapter and paragraph divisions. It may also give you a new perspective. The three parts to a simple horizontal chart are: 1) The Major Divisions of the Book, 2) Chapter Titles, and 3) Paragraph Titles. See the sample form at the end of this chapter to learn how to make a horizontal chart.

1. Create as many columns, as there are chapters in the book.

2. Reread the book. At the top of your chart record each major division, in as few words as possible.

3. Reread the book once again, this time creating a title for each chapter (or group of chapters in a longer book). Record these at the top of each column directly below the major divisions. Two characteristics for good chapter titles are:

   • Preferably, use no more than four words.

   • Use picturesque words that help you visualize it.

4. Reread the book once again, this time titling every paragraph. Try to connect the paragraph titles to each chapter's title.

Step 5 Make a detailed outline of the book

Outline the main points and show their relationship to one another. Your outline should flow from the major to the minor. List major divisions first, followed by subdivisions (which could also be the chapters), and finally, the important points that fall under each subdivision (which could also be the paragraphs). Refer to your horizontal chart to help you create your outline. And, just for fun, compare your outline with other outlines that you find in commentaries. It is interesting to get other perspectives.

Step 6 Develop a personal application

The main purpose of a book survey is to help you get acquainted with the general contents of the book you are studying. However, since one goal of every Bible study is application, you should make note of ways you can personally apply the biblical insights you discover. Select one principle that the Lord revealed during your study time and write how that truth can be applied in your life.

The next page has a sample of the Book Details Bible study method.

BOOK DETAILS

SCRIPTURE - Habakkuk
TIMES READ - 2

NOTES ON WHAT I READ
- My first impression is that this prophet has boldness to talk to God like that! I love how God allows the conversation and humors him by letting him in on His plan. That's crazy!
- Words repeated most - faith, woe
- Emotional tone of author - panic, doubt, eventually trust
- Logical argument - God is sovereign, so don't worry
- Literary style - dialogue and song

BACKGROUND STUDY
- Author - Habakkuk - involved in temple worship
- Date written - ??? During Babylonian era (before captivity)
- To whom written - Judah
- Key verse - 1:3 - "live by faith!"
- Purpose - to remind Habakkuk and all readers that God is in control and should be trusted even during dark times when He "feels" absent.
- Source - Thompson Chain Reference Bible

HORIZONTAL CHART

The Book of Habakkuk		
Problems of Habakkuk		Praise of Habakkuk
ch. 1:1-2:1	ch. 2:2-20	ch. 3
A Prophet's Question	God is Just	A Prophet's Prayer
1:1-4 Habakkuk's First Question	2:2-4 Live by Faith 2:5-19 Babylonian Judgement	3:1-16 Remembering God's Faithful
1:5-11 God's First Reply		3:17-19 Praise God During Storms
1:12-2:1 Habakkuk's Second Question	2:20 God is in Control	

DETAILED OUTLINE

I. The Problems of Habakkuk (1:1-2:20)
   A. Habakkuk's First Problem (1:1-4)
   B. God's First Response (1:5-11)
   C. Habakkuk's Second Problem (1:12-2:1)
   D. God's Second Response (2:2-20)
II. The Praise of Habakkuk (3:1-19)
   A. The Prophet Prays For God's Mercy (3:1-2)
   B. The Prophet Remembers God's Faithfulness (3:3-15)
   C. The Prophet Praise God In Trial (3:16-19)

APPLICATION — Habakkuk 3:17-19

Times are tough now financially in my house. I need to rejoice in the Lord despite my trial because God is in control. To find the strength to rejoice, I will dialogue with my God like Habakkuk did (Hebrews 4:16).

Bible Characters

Our English word "biography" comes from two Greek words that mean "life-writing." Dr. Douglas Southall Freeman said, "Men read biography, I think, primarily because they live it. When they peruse history, they are onlookers, but when they study a life, they participate in it." The same can be said of the study of biblical characters. As we turn the pages of Scripture, we learn how God molds His children and how they respond to Him. The practical and personal implications of character studies such as these are important lessons to Christians today. We learn who we are and how we are to live by both observing and emulating the positive attributes of biblical men and women, and avoiding the tremendous failures and negative aspects in the lives of those who did not heed God's Word.

When you decide to study the life of a biblical character, begin by researching the Scriptures that relate to his or her life. As you study, seek to become thoroughly acquainted with that person and their personal struggles. Find out what made them a spiritual success or failure. Ask God to help you to be able to discern how they were thinking or feeling as you study the circumstances surrounding their lives, and begin applying what you learn from their example to your own areas of weakness.

God gave us the stories in the Old Testament so that they would be examples to us (1 Corinthians 10:11). New Testament truths are often illustrated in the lives of those who lived during the Old Testament period. Though both testaments contain instructions and illustrations, the New Testament is predominantly a book of instruction, while the Old Testament contains more illustrations. So, one of the best ways to study the Old Testament is to look at the lives of its people. Biographical studies are enjoyable and are one of the easiest methods from which to find personal applications.

Some Tips to Keep in Mind for a Good Character Study

- Start with someone on whom you can do a simple study. Do not start with a person whose life-story has a large amount of information such as Jesus, Moses, or Abraham.

- Get inside their mind. Try to imagine how they were thinking, feeling, and responding to their circumstances. Put yourself in the story—attempt to see through their eyes, hear with their ears, mingle with their friends, and fight with their enemies.

- Don't confuse people and their stories just because they have the same name. For example, there are thirty different men named Zechariah in the Bible, twenty named Nathan, seven women named Mary, and five men with the name of John. Be sure to check the context or a topical Bible to be certain that you are not mixing them up.

- Various names may apply to certain people. For example, the apostle Peter is referred to as Simon, Simeon, and Cephas, in different passages. So, when you are doing a character study, be diligent to find every reference, even those that may contain a different name.

- Do your own work first then check other sources. Stay away from books written about biblical people until you have exhausted every Bible reference about that person.

Complete the following steps to do a *Bible Character* study:

Step 1 Select the Bible person you want to study

There are 2,930 men and women mentioned in the Bible. You might start out by selecting someone who either has a weakness that you can identify with, or a strength that you would like to develop. It might be interesting to begin a study of a certain group of characters, such as: friends of Jesus, servants mentioned in the Bible, those who have failed, or the greatest conversions in the Bible.

Step 2 Compile a list of every biblical reference

Find all the passages in Scripture about the person you are studying and everything related to his/her life. Use the cross-references in the margins of your Bible, a topical Bible, or an exhaustive concordance to help you put the list together.

Step 3 Write your first impressions

List basic observations and important information that you discover about him or her. Do not overlook any detail, no matter how small. Every fact adds color and depth, and when taken into consideration together, often proves significant.

Step 4 Make a timeline

Review all the references and make a chronological outline of the person's life. This will help you see how different life events relate to one another. Look for any major changes in his or her life, record any progressions and shifts in attitude. Doing this will help you see how they either allowed God to mold and transform their lives through their circumstances, or how they gave Satan a foothold that eventually destroyed them.

Step 5 Ask questions

You don't have to answer all of these questions, but after reviewing your references choose ten of these that would be helpful to answer?

- What was his/her physical description?
- What was his/her conversion experience?
- What did people say about him/her?
- Did he/she write any portion of Scripture?
- Who were his/her enemies and what did they say?
- What did God say about him/her?
- How did he/she respond to failure?
- Did he/she get discouraged?
- How did he/she respond to adversity?
- Did he/she handle criticism well?
- How did he/she respond to success?
- How quickly did he/she obey God when told to do something?

- What can you discover about his/her family and <u>ancestry</u>?
- What does his/her <u>name mean</u>? Was it ever changed?
- What were the <u>characteristics of his/her parents</u>?
- Did any of them <u>rub off</u> on their children?
- Where did he/she <u>live</u>?
- Was there anything special about his/her <u>birth</u>?
- What was the <u>spiritual and political</u> condition of their country?
- What was his/her <u>occupation</u>?
- What would his/her <u>job be today</u>?
- <u>How long</u> did he/she live?
- Where and how did he/she <u>die</u>?
- Was there any <u>great crisis</u> in his/her life? How was it handled?
- What are his/her memorable <u>accomplishments</u>?
- Did he/she experience a <u>divine call</u> from God?
- How did they <u>respond</u> to God's call to service?
- Was there any <u>recurring problem</u> in his/her life?
- What part did he/she play in the history of <u>God's plan</u>?
- What was his/her general <u>attitude</u> toward life and others?
- How did he/she <u>get along</u> with other people?
- What was his/her <u>family</u> like? (Wife/husband/parents/children)
- Who were his/her <u>close friends</u>? Did they influence him/her?
- What <u>influence</u> did he/she have on others? On the nation?
- Did he/she <u>train anyone</u> to take his/her place?
- What were his/her particular <u>weaknesses</u>?
- What were his/her particular <u>sins</u>?
- What <u>steps</u> led to those sins?
- What were the <u>results of his/her sins</u> and weaknesses?
- Did he/she <u>ever get victory</u> over particular sins?
- What was his/her <u>spiritual status</u>?

- Carefully determine his/her <u>religious experiences</u> (prayer/service/ knowledge of Scripture).

- What was the person's <u>relation to Christ</u> (as a type, forerunner, believer, enemy, servant, brother, friend, etc.)

- Did his/her life show any <u>development of character</u> over time?

Step 6 Identify some personal characteristics

Review the Scripture references again and use the suggested list below of positive and negative characteristics as a checklist. Give a verse reference that shows each characteristic you have observed in the person you are studying.

<u>A Partial List of Positive (Godly) Character Traits</u>

Servant, Agreeable, Balanced, Bold, Brave, Calm, Careful, Cautious, Characterized by the Beatitudes, Chaste, Cheerful, Clean, Compassionate, Confident, Considerate, Content, Courageous, Courteous, Creative, Dedicated, Dependable, Determinate, Diligent, Discerning, Disciplined, Discreet, Durable, Earnest, Energetic, Enthusiastic, Fair, Faithful, Flexible Forgiving, Generous, Gentle, Good Steward, Grateful, Honest, Humble, Independent, Industrious, Integrity, Kind, Loving, Loyal, Meek, Merciful, Moderate, Modest, Obedient, Optimistic, Orderly, Patient, Peacemaker, Positive, Pure, Quiet, Resourceful, Respectful, Reverent, Righteous, Sacrificial, Self-controlled, Self-denying, Self-giving, Sense of Humor Sensitivity, Sincerity, Stable, Submissive, Sympathetic, Thankful, Thrifty, Tolerant, Trustworthy, Uncomplaining, Uncompromising, Wholehearted, Wise, Zealous.

<u>A Partial List of Negative (Ungodly) Character Traits</u>

A Busybody, A Cop-out, A Doubter, A Drunkard, A Liar, A Sluggard, A Worrier, Adulterous, Angry Without Cause, Annoying, Apathetic, Apostate, Argumentative, Arrogant, Ashamed of Christ, Backbiter, Bigoted, Bitter, Blasphemous, Boastful, Callous, Careless, Coarse, Complaining, Compromising, Conceited, Covetous, Cowardly, Crafty/ Sly, Cruel, Deceitful, Dishonest, Disobedient, Disrespectful, Doctrinally Off, Dogmatic, Double-minded, Envious, Fearful, Fears Men, Flatterer, Foolish, Forgetful, Fornicator, Friend of the World, Gluttonous, Gossiper, Greedy, Grudging, Halfhearted, Harsh, Humorless, Hypocritical, Idle, Idolatrous, Immodest, Immoral, Impolite, Impulsive, Independent Spirit, Indifferent, Insulting, Irritating, Jealous, Lazy, Legalistic, Lukewarm,

Lusts for Power, Malicious, Manipulative, Negligent, Prejudiced, Presumptuous, Procrastinator, Profane, Proud, Rebellious, Rejoices in Evil, Reprobate, Rude/Gross, Sarcastic, Scornful, Self-righteous, Selfish, Shallow, Shortsighted, Slanderer, Stingy, Stubborn, Talkative, Tyrannical, Unclean, Undisciplined, Unfair, Unfaithful, Unforgiving, Ungrateful, Unkind, Unreliable, Unsociable, Vain, Violent, Wasteful, Worldly.

Step 7 Other Bible truths illustrated in this person

Does this person's life illustrate other truths taught in the Bible? Maybe some wisdom in the Proverbs relates to this story or a New Testament principle. Find and list cross-references to back up your thoughts.

Step 8 Summarize the main lesson and keywords

Summarize what you believe are the main lessons taught or illustrated in this person's life. Try to find at least one major weakness (or bad example) that you want to avoid in your own life, and one major strength (or good example) that you would like to emulate. Is there one word that could describe his or her life? What one personal characteristic stands out?

Make this study portable by familiarizing yourself with the details of each of the main lessons you learned. Then begin sharing the entire life story of this character with others, emphasizing that main lesson.

Step 9 Write a personal application

Ask yourself some of these questions:

- Did I see anything of myself in this person's life (bad or good)?
- What impressed me the most about this person's life?
- Where am I lacking when it comes to these godly characteristics and what will I do about it?

The next page has a sample of the Bible Characters Bible study method.

BIBLE CHARACTERS

NAME - Caleb

REFERENCES - Numbers 13:6, Numbers 32:12, Joshua 14 + 15, Judges 1:12-15, Judges 3:9

FIRST IMPRESSIONS
- Caleb was one of the 12 spies sent by Moses.
- Only Caleb and Joshua believed the promises of God
- Caleb wholly followed the Lord his God
- Caleb still had great strength at age 85
- Caleb conquered a mountain

TIMELINE
1. Caleb sent into Canaan to spy out the land
2. Caleb commended for his trust in God.
3. Caleb conquers mountain at age 85!

QUESTIONS
Q. Who were his enemies? A. The Anakim- giants!
Q. What was the spiritual condition of his country?
A. At first, horrible as they rebelled against God, later with Joshua as their leader, it improved.
Q. What part did he play in the history of God's plan?
A. Caleb was a leader at the foundation of the nation He helped to possess the promised land in war.
Q. What was his family like?
A. Daughter was wise and son in law was courageous

CHARACTERISTICS
- confidence (Joshua 14:11) • fearless (Joshua 15:14)
- generous (Joshua 15:19) • faithful (Joshua 14:19)
- courageous (Joshua 14:12)

OTHER TRUTHS
- He believed in and trusted the promises of God, as Romans 4:13-25 talks about.
- He didn't let anything get in the way of his obeying God's call, like Acts 5:29 shows.

MAIN LESSON
Main Lesson – Wholly follow God no matter what the cost is.
Keyword – confidence (in God's Word)
Characteristics – Regardless of what others said or did, Caleb trusted God

PERSONAL APPLICATION
I hope to become more confident, like Caleb was. He knew God's Word and acted upon it with unwavering obedience. I'm going to find a promise that relates to a struggle I have and memorize it today so I'll be ready next time I'm tempted.

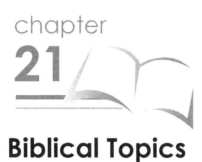

chapter

21

Biblical Topics

One of the most exciting ways to study the Bible is by examining it topically. Doing so allows us to study subjects that are of particular interest. Biblical topics usually have many minor themes running through them. In order to do a topical study, every related passage should be considered. The *Biblical Topics* method will help you to select the subject matter, trace it through the entire Bible, and discover everything that God has said about it, in His Word.

The *Biblical Topics* method can be used to study a doctrine, an idea, a phrase, or any subject that is mentioned in the Bible. It enables us to study the Word of God systematically, logically, and in an orderly manner. It gives us a proper balance regarding biblical truth as we get to see the whole counsel of God's Word on the subject. To keep you on course let's look at some helpful hints before we start.

Suggestions for a Good Topical Study

R. A. Torrey, a great Bible teacher, gives three suggestions that are helpful in studying the Bible topically. They are as follows:

1. <u>Be systematic</u>. Never study the Bible haphazardly. Make a list of all the subjects that are related to your topic. Be as comprehensive and complete as possible. Then take these items one at a time, studying them in a systematic and logical order.

2. Be thorough. Do your best to find and study every verse that relates to the topic. The only way to know everything that God has said on a topic is to go through the entire Bible and find all the passages on that topic. You will need to use a concordance to do this.

3. Be exact. Study each verse in order to understand its exact meaning. Be sure to examine the context of each verse in order to avoid misinterpretation. The biggest mistake you must avoid in doing a topical study is taking a verse out of its context.

With that in mind, complete the following steps to get started on a *Biblical Topics* study:

Step 1 Choose a topic that interests you

Is there a biblical topic that you would like to study—one that excites you or maybe one that has always confused you? It may be a topic that was specifically mentioned in a passage that you read in your daily reading and you want to learn more about it. Or maybe it was something that was just merely implied in a text but it is of special personal interest to you, so you want to dig into it a little further.

Step 2 Create a list of words

Make a list of all the related words, synonyms, phrases, and anything else that could have something to do with your topic. This will help you search the Bible more completely for God's thoughts on that topic.

Step 3 Collect verse references

Gather all the verses you can find on the topic by looking up each related word in a concordance. You will also want to use a topical Bible to get references that may relate in thought but not in word. Be sure to look for illustrations as well. For example, on a study on the topic of faith you might include stories about Abraham and Rahab.

Step 4 Consider each reference individually

Read and study every reference, write down your observations and insights on each verse. Be sure to check the context carefully so that your interpretation will be correct. Define all the key words that you come across (use a Bible dictionary). Ask as many questions as you can about each verse in order to find the intended meaning. Remember to use the what, why, when, where, who, and how questions.

Step 5 Compare and group the references into themes

After you have carefully studied all the verses individually, you will begin to notice that some of the references naturally complement each other and deal with the same themes of the topic under study. Categorize these references on a piece of scratch paper for now.

Step 6 Condense your study into an outline

Outline your study by arranging the themes logically under main divisions. Do this by grouping related or similar references together under different theme divisions.

Step 7 Concluding thoughts

Summarize your findings in a brief paragraph. What have you learned about this topic? How have the themes you've found broadened your understanding of the Biblical perspective on this topic?

Step 8 Application

Write a practical application drawn from your concluding summary. Identify one area of your life where you can better live out these truths. Make a plan and give yourself a deadline.

The next page has a sample of the Biblical Topics Bible study method. (Note: A true topical Bible study will be exhaustive in reviewing every applicable verse. I've limited this example to just enough verses to give you the general idea of how to complete a topical study.)

BIBLICAL TOPICS

TOPIC - Giving
WORDS - offering, gift, firstfruits, tenth, giving, tithe

VERSES - (Search limited to New Testament)
• Matthew 19:21 - We must be willing to part with earthly riches. A heavenly treasure is promised to givers.

• Matthew 23:23 - Tithing must accompany godly living.

• Luke 21:1-4 - It's not about how much you give, it's your heart. This widow trusted in God's provision.

• 2 Corinthians 9:2-3 - Get excited about giving.

• 2 Corinthians 9:8 - Give cheerfully.

• 1 Corinthians 16:2 - Plan to give (at church).

• Matthew 6:2-4 - Give secretly and let God reward.

• Matthew 6:19-21 - Giving is one of the ways that we store up treasure in heaven.

• Acts 5:1-11 - Give with the right motives.

OUTLINE
The heart behind giving must be pure.
- Matthew 23:23
- Acts 5:1-11

God wants a joyful giver.
- 2 Corinthians 9:2-3
- 2 Corinthians 9:8

There is a reward for giving.
- Matthew 6:2-3
- Matthew 6:19-21

Giving helps us to trust God.
- Matthew 19:21
- Luke 21:1-4

Giving should be consistent.
- 1 Corinthians 16:2

CONCLUSION - Giving is for my own good. It helps me to "give" away my greediness. It helps me practically to be more trusting in God, to provide for me as I give back to Him.

APPLICATION - I am going to save $10 weekly for ten weeks and then give that money towards sponsoring a student to go on the winter retreat.

chapter

22

Bible Themes

This Bible study method helps you determine themes within the Scriptures. Themes are different than topics. They are specific ideas within a larger topical thought. For instance, in the topic of "prayer" two separate themes are: "the prayers of Jesus" and "the conditions of answered prayer." When doing a thematic study, you first need to decide on a set of questions to ask about the chosen theme before looking into a book of the Bible or the entire Bible.

The thematic study, while similar to the topical study, differs in two ways:

1. <u>The thematic study involves fewer verses</u>. A topical study would examine every possible verse that relates to the overall topic. In a thematic study, you concentrate only on passages of Scripture that deal with your selected theme.

2. <u>A thematic study entails fewer questions</u>. In a topical study you ask as many questions as you can, because your goal is to discover as much as possible about the topic. However, in a thematic study a limit is set of no more than five carefully chosen questions. After making a list of all the verses related to the theme, you examine each verse, asking only the questions you have prepared. Sometimes you can do a thematic study with only one question, such as, "What are the things God hates?" or "What traits of a fool are given in the book of Proverbs?"

Complete the following steps to get started on a *Bible Themes* study:

Step 1 Choose a theme

Select a specific theme (not a topic) in which you are interested. If you have not done a study of this kind before, choose a theme that is relatively simple.

Step 2 List all the verses you intend to study

Using an exhaustive concordance and a topical Bible make a list of all the Scripture verses that are related to the theme you have chosen. Remember to consider synonyms and other similar words and concepts when using the concordance. From this list, select only the verses that are most important to your theme.

Step 3 Decide on the questions

How do you know what questions to ask? Simple. What are some of the things you would like to know about your theme? Make a list of those questions (not more than five in number). And remember, sometimes you may only want to ask one question. Here's an example using the theme of anger in the Book of Proverbs:

- What are the characteristics of an angry man?
- What causes anger?
- What are the results of anger?
- What is the cure for anger?

All four of these questions begin with the word, "what" but you could come up with just as many questions using the other five question starters: Why? When? Where? Who? How?

Step 4 Ask your questions of each reference

Ask the same questions of each referenced verse and write down your answers. You may not find an answer to every one of your questions in each verse. Just leave a blank space on your form and move on to the next question. If you are not finding answers to any of your questions, it probably means you are asking the wrong questions. Reread the verses and try again.

Step 5 Draw some conclusions from your study

After you have finished checking the references and writing your answers, go back and summarize the answers to each of your questions. You might organize your study into an outline by grouping similar verses together and turning your questions into the major divisions of the outline.

Step 6 Write a personal application

To implement what you have discovered and make it real in your life, write a personal application.

The next page has a sample of the Bible Themes Bible study method.

BIBLICAL THEMES

THEMES - The Things That God Hates

VERSES - Proverbs 6:16-19, Psalm 11:5, Zechariah 8:17, Isaiah 61:8, Malachi 2:16, Revelation 2:6, Amos 5:21

QUESTIONS TO ASK
1) What does God hate?
2) Why does God hate these things?
3) Who does God hate?

ANSWERS TO QUESTIONS
1) What does God hate?
- Proverbs 6:16-19 - a proud look, a lying tongue, hands that shed innocent blood, a heart that devises wicked plans, feet swift to run to evil, a false witness who speaks lies, one who sows discord among the brethren.
- Psalm 11:5 - one who loves violence.
- Zechariah 8:17 - thinking evil against your neighbor.
- Isaiah 61:8 - robbery.
- Malachi 2:16 - divorce
- Revelation 2:6 - the deeds of the Nicolaitans.
- Amos 5:21 - false worship ("dead religion")

2) Why does God hate these things?
- Proverbs 6:16-19 — this describes an enemy of God.
- Psalm 11:5 — violence hurts God's children.
- Zechariah 8:17 — thinking evil of neighbor violates their trust of you.
- Isaiah 61:8 — robbery is selfish and God provides.
- Malachi 2:16 — divorce ruins the picture of Jesus being married to the church.
- Revelation 2:6 — Nicolaitans were corrupting the church
- Amos 5:21 — False worship is hypocritical

3) Who does God hate?
- Psalm 11:5 — the wicked, because God's wrath is against sin, only Jesus saves from this.

CONCLUSIONS
God hates these things because they are sin. I should search my heart and examine my life for any of these things to make sure I am pleasing God.

APPLICATION
Because God hates these things, I ought to hate them as well. To help my attitude, I won't make jokes about sinful situations anymore. That only causes me to take those things lightly.

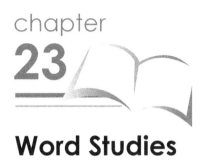

chapter

23

Word Studies

The Bible is the Word of God so, naturally, word studies are an important way of learning more about the message God originally communicated to us in His Word. This method of Bible study helps us discover the rich meaning of the original texts, which were written in the ancient Hebrew, Aramaic, and Greek languages. In the past, those who were interested in doing biblical word studies needed a working knowledge of those archaic languages. However, today biblical word studies are within the reach of every Christian who knows the right tools to use to help them discover the richness of the original text.

The purpose of doing word studies is to learn the intended meaning that was being conveyed by the writer as precisely and comprehensively as possible. The correct interpretation of biblical truth always depends on how well we understand what the writer meant. Word studies help us to understand that meaning a little better because they reveal why he chose one word over another.

How does knowing which specific ancient word was used in the original text help our understanding of the Bible today? It's been said that approximately 8,674 different Hebrew words were used in the Old Testament, while some 5,624 different Greek words were used to write the New Testament. However, the English translation consists of only about 6,000 different English words in the Old and New Testaments combined. So how did they squeeze the original 14,298 different words into the 6,000 different words we have in our Bibles? They did it by using the same

English word to translate several different words in the original language. Therefore, while our English translation of the Bible is an accurate and complete rendering of the contents of the original texts, it lacks some of the more subtle shades of meaning that are understood in the original language. Word studies are profitable because they help us to understand the full spectrum of meaning that the original language conveys.

As with every other method of Bible study, word studies are most useful when they are observed in the context of the surrounding verses. When a word's specific definition is applied to the context of the passage, the full meaning of the text can be known and applied correctly.

Two Things to Remember About Word Studies

1. Word studies must be based on the original language words, not on the English words. For instance: we won't be studying the definition of English words such as "truth." Instead we will be looking for the original definition of the Hebrew or Greek word that was translated into the English word "truth."

2. We must always allow the context to dictate the ultimate meaning of the word being studied no matter what the English equivalent might be.

Tools You Will Need

For this method of Bible study, you will need more reference tools than you have used with other methods. The necessary tools are: a study Bible, several recent translations (do not use paraphrases), an exhaustive concordance, a Bible dictionary and/or encyclopedia, a set of Biblical word studies, and a good English dictionary.

Four Difficulties That Are Common in Word Studies

As you begin this method of Bible study, you need to be aware of some difficulties that might arise.

1. Several different Greek words are translated into one English word. Be sure to check your concordance carefully to see if this is true of the word you are studying.

2. One Greek or Hebrew word can be translated several ways in English. To overcome this difficulty you will have to do a careful study on all the different English renderings of the original word.

When you come across this issue follow these guidelines to help you find the original language word:

- List the different ways the word is translated. How often?

- Give examples of each translation (if possible).

- Write down how the different meanings are related.

- Determine if the writer of the book is using the word you are studying, in a single sense or is giving it a multiple meaning.

3. <u>An original word can be translated by a whole English phrase</u>. A concordance does not list word translations by phrases. You will have to compare the recent versions of the Bible you are using to see how the various translators have rendered the word.

4. <u>Language syntax can be complicated</u>. Understanding how words are put together grammatically requires knowing the rules that determine the true meaning and correct usage of a word. A good word study resource will help you overcome this difficulty.

Complete the following steps to do a *Word Study* Bible study:

Step 1 Choose the word you want to study within a verse

It should be an important biblical word. Write the word and the specific verse that you found it in. Read the verse a few times in context.

Step 2 Find its English definition

Use your regular English dictionary and write out the definition of the word. Make note of the definition and any synonyms or antonyms. A Bible dictionary is not the same as a regular dictionary. A regular dictionary gives the meaning of the words as they are currently used. A Bible dictionary gives the definition of Bible words as they were used in the original context of Scripture.

Step 3 Compare translations

Read the verse in different recent translations and write down how it is rendered in each of them. Keep track of which rendering is used most commonly in these translations.

Step 4 Write a short definition of the Hebrew or Greek word

Find out what word was used in the original language by using an exhaustive concordance or word study book and write down its short definition. Also, make note of the Strong's number for future reference.

Step 5 Check the word's occurrences in the Bible

Using a concordance, research how and where the word is used in the Bible. Ask these questions:

- How many <u>times</u> does the word occur in the Bible?
- In which <u>books</u> does it occur?
- In which book does it <u>occur most</u>?
- Where does the word <u>occur first</u> in the Bible?
- Where does it <u>occur first in the book</u> I am studying?

Step 6 Research a longer definition

This step takes a little research to complete. You will want to read a fuller description of the meaning and origin of the word you are studying using a Bible dictionary, a Bible encyclopedia, or a word study set. Find the <u>root meaning</u> and the <u>etymology</u> (history) of the Hebrew or Greek word.

Step 7 Discover the word's usage in the Bible

How is the word used in the Scriptures? The study of the root meaning (from step 6) provides a definition of what the word originally meant and where it came from. But the meaning of some words changes over time. And some words have a different meaning depending upon the situation or context. In the final analysis, the usage of a word is the most important factor in determining its true meaning. Fulfill this step in the following three ways:

1. Using an exhaustive concordance, find out <u>how the Hebrew or Greek word is translated into English every time it appears</u> in the Bible. Write the amount of times that particular English word is used.

2. <u>Learn this word's contribution and function</u> in the context of an isolated verse, paragraph, or chapter. You can ask some or all of the following questions:
   - How does the writer use it in other parts of the book?

- How does the writer use it in other books he has written?
- How is the word used throughout the whole Testament?
- How is it used the first time in the Scriptures?
- What is the most frequent use of the word?
- What would we know about this topic if this verse was the only mention of it in Scripture?

NOTE: Additional research can be performed on Hebrew Old Testament words by finding the correlating Greek word that was used in the Septuagint (LXX) translation. This will allow you to research that particular Greek word in the New Testament for further understanding.

3. <u>Find out how the word is used in the context of the passage</u>. This is the ultimate test. The context will be your most reliable source for insights into what the writer meant to convey. Ask:

- Does the context give any clues to the word's meaning?
- Is the word compared or contrasted with another word?
- Is there any illustration in the context that clarifies it?

Step 8 Bring the word's meaning back to the verse

Now that you've discovered the original meaning for this word, read the verse once again, substituting the expanded definition into the context. Does the new meaning add light to the verse? Make a list of how the new meaning helps you to better understand this particular verse.

Step 9 Write an application

When doing a word study, be careful to remember that the goal of your study is application, not interpretation only. Remember that you are doing personal Bible study, not just conducting an academic exercise. Constantly ask, "How can understanding this word strengthen my spiritual life?"

It is encouraging to know that the words which God inspired in the original languages have not been watered down over the centuries in the translation process. With this study method you no longer have to say, "it's all Greek to me!" Visit http://www.LearnToStudyTheBible.com to use free online tools to help you complete a step-by-step word study.

The next page has a sample of the Word Studies Bible study method.

WORD STUDY

WORD - clean
SCRIPTURE - Psalm 51:10
"create in me a clean heart, O God."

ENGLISH DEFINITION - Adjective;
free from dirt, unsoiled, unstained. In a
spiritual sense-morally pure, innocent, upright.

COMPARE TRANSLATIONS
• "pure" (NIV, CEV)
• "clean" (NJKV, KJV, ESV, NLT, NASB)

STRONG'S NUMBER - H2889

SHORT DEFINITION OF HEBREW WORD
"tahor"(adj.) clean, pure, flawless, moral

OCCURANCES IN BIBLE
• Times used - 95 times
• Books that use it - Ge, Le, Nu, De, 1S, 2Chr,
  Jb, Ps, Ec, Is, Eze
• Where it occurs most - Leviticus
• Where it occurs first - Genesis 7:2
• Where it appears first in the book that I'm
  studying - Psalm 19:9

LONGER DEFINITION - Several times, tahor is used of physical purity, mainly of gold (Ex 25:11). It is derived from the verb taher (H2881), "to be pure". It is also used of the moral, spiritual purity of God's words (Ps 12:6) and eyes (Hab 1:13).

The common use of this word is the theological concept of fitness or qualification for the presence of the Holy God. Uncleanness would prevent the worshiper from approaching the Lord or being part of the community.

Clean versus unclean uses the image of impurity for the effects of the sin problem in the world. David prayed for God to create in him a "clean" heart in parallel with making a new determination within him to do what is right and not casting him away from God's presence (Ps. 51:10)
[Def. taken from Unger's Bible Dictionary]

BIBLE USAGE
• The English words used for this Hebrew word- clean[5], pure[40], fair[2], pureness[1], power[1]
• Within the same book of Psalms "clean" is used as a characteristic of God's Word in Ps 12:6 and Ps 19:9 describing the Word's purity/flawlessness.
• In Exodus "pure" describes the pureness of gold.
• Places can be "clean" (Le 10:14)
• Ceremonially "clean" people could eat offerings (Nu 18:13)
• Uncleanness causes separation (De 23:10)

· A woman caught in adultery is "unclean" (Nu 5:28)
· In Habakkuk "pure" describes God's eyes
· The first time this word appears in the
Bible (Ge 7:2) is in reference to animals
being "clean" or not, as described further in
the law.

Septuagint Greek word used - Strong's #G2513
"katharos" (adj.) - clean, pure - physically in a
levitical sense, and ethically. Used 28 times
in the New Testament.
· The "pure" in heart shall see God (Mt 5:8).
· Jesus used foot washing as an illustration
of the spiritual cleansing that is needed (Jn 13:10)
· God's Word cleanses us (Jn 15:3).
· "Pure" white shows a picture of holiness (Re 15:6).

Context Clues to Meaning
Psalm 51 was written by David after he was
caught in adultery by Nathan the prophet. It
is a Psalm of repentance. David must feel
dirty from his sin because he asks to be
"washed" by God.

[BACK TO THE VERSE] - Psalm 51:10
David's sin caused him to feel seperate from
God (Ps 51:11) - defilement does this (De 23:10).
Since only the "pure in heart" see God (Mt 5:8),
David wants God to wash him (Ps 51:7),
which happens by God's Word (Jn 15:3). This

new clean heart would restore fellowship with God (Nu 18:13). God would have to create this clean heart for David because by human standards he was guilty (Nu 5:28).

APPLICATION

I realize that my sin is making me dirty and it causes separation from God. I must also beg God for a clean heart that is free from the impurity of sinful memories. I will renew my mind by bathing myself in His Word daily.

CREATIVE BIBLE STUDY METHODS

Interesting Methods that Add
Variety to Bible Study

These methods are meant to add flavor and variety to any Bible study. Occasionally mixing in a few of these interesting approaches to the study of God's Word will sharpen your spiritual senses and help you grow in your understanding of the Scriptures. They will cause you to think creatively about the text you are reading, and experience its truth in ways you may never have before.

chapter

24

Translation Comparison

We all have our favorite Bible translation: the one that we use most frequently to study the Scriptures. But, our understanding of any biblical passage is enhanced when we read it in more than one translation. This Bible study method will help you learn how to compare the Scriptures using other accurate translations of the Bible.

Every translation is the work of a group of scholars—it is the culmination of years of experience in language skills and dedicated research efforts. Different translations can be fun to read and usually increase our understanding of the truths being expressed through their different renderings. When we read a verse in a number of different translations, the result is similar to using a commentary, except it has the benefit of keeping our focus on the Scripture alone.

Many Translations Are Available Today. My Suggestions Are:

1. The King James Version (KJV): For almost four hundred years the King James Version (also referred to as the Authorized Version), was the prominent translation used in most Protestant churches. It is a word-for-word translation (or a formal equivalent) originally published in 1611 at the request of King James I of England.

2. The New King James Version (NKJV): This popular version is a modern word-for-word translation and retains the purity and stylistic beauty of the original King James Version.

3. <u>The English Standard Version</u> (ESV): This is essentially a literal Bible translation that combines word-for-word precision and accuracy with literary excellence, beauty, and depth of meaning.

4. <u>The Amplified Bible</u> (AMP): This translation is very useful in understanding the different meanings of words right within the text. Parentheses and dashes are used to include additional phrases of meaning. Brackets are used to contain clarifying words or commentary that may or may not be implied, but are not expressed in the original language.

5. <u>The New International Version</u> (NIV): This is an easy-to-read new translation by evangelical scholars. It is a balance between a word-for-word translation and a thought-for-thought paraphrase.

6. <u>New Living Translation</u> (NLT): This is a thought-for-thought paraphrase rather than a translation. In a paraphrase, the author translates the main thought from the original into our contemporary language. However, sometimes entirely different expressions are used in order to convey a clearer and fuller explanation that can be more easily understood today. Doctrine should never be based on a paraphrase; only a more accurate word-for-word translation should be used when it comes to understanding biblical precepts.

Is It Necessary to Buy Five New Bibles?

It is not necessary to buy a number of different Bible translations in order to be able to do this method of Bible study. You can use either a parallel Bible, which contains a few different translations, or you can search the Internet. Many websites allow you to quickly compare different Bible translations on your computer. For a free translation comparison tool visit our website at http://www.LearnToStudyTheBible.com.

Follow These Rules to Keep Your Study Accurate

1. Rely upon the <u>Holy Spirit</u> to guide your study and understanding of Scripture (John 14:26 and 16:13).

2. Regardless of the translation, meaning must be judged on the basis of <u>context</u>.

3. Compare the translation to the <u>general teaching</u> in other passages of Scripture.

4. Do not seek variety just for the sake of <u>variety</u>. Some words are translated into one English word because it is the best word.

5. The <u>majority</u> is not always right, but should influence you.

6. In your personal expanded translation or paraphrase, <u>use brackets</u> to enclose words or comments that are not in the text. In this way you can have a mixture of translation and commentary.

Follow these steps to begin a *Translation Comparison* Bible study:

Step 1 Read each verse in the version you regularly use

I would recommend that every Bible student use a modern, word-for-word translation (NKJV, NASB, or ESV).

Step 2 Read the same verse in other translations

If any version renders a word, phrase, or sentence with greater under-standing and meaning, it should be considered. In the appropriate box, write only the variations that you think are important to your study.

Repeat steps one and two with each verse in the studied passage.

Step 3 Write your personal expanded paraphrase

Do this on the back of the sheet of paper. Remember to put brackets around any comments or explanations that are not actually in the text. You can expect that your version will not flow as smoothly as regular translations, but it should be packed with special meaning for you.

Step 4 Read your expanded translation and title it

You now should have acquired an understanding of the passage that you didn't have when you began. Try to digest this understanding into a short title for the passage, and then write this title on the chart.

Step 5 Application

It has been said that the best translation of Scripture is when it is translated into our every day life. After having studied this verse and with the help of all the scholarly wisdom that went into making all the translations you used, what are you going to do with what you have learned? What obedience does God require of you today? Plan an application and give yourself a date to complete it.

The next page has a sample of the Translation Comparison Bible study.

TRANSLATION COMPARISON

SCRIPTURE - Jeremiah 29:11

NKJV	KJV	NLT	NIV
For I know the thoughts		For I know the plans	
that I think toward you		I have for you	
says the Lord	saith the Lord		declares the Lord
thoughts of peace		they are plans for good	plans to prosper you
and not of evil		and not for disaster	and not to harm you
to give you			
a future and a hope	an expected end		

PERSONAL TRANSLATION

Yes I [God] know [all about] the plans [for your life] that I've made for you [Andy]. I'm God [so listen]. [great] plans with your best interest in mind, not bad plans [I am not against you], but plans that give you the best final outcome, so have hope [and trust in me].

TITLE - God's Goodness Guaranteed

APPLICATION
God really does ALWAYS have my best in mind. So I need to trust Him during the storms. This is good news and if I believe it I should rejoice. I'm going to smile more today than I have in weeks no matter what happens!

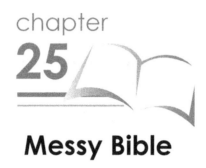

chapter

25

Messy Bible

In a *Messy Bible* study, you will highlight, mark, underline, draw symbols, and color the Scripture so much, that it will become alive to you in a new way. There is something about all that hands-on participation with Scripture that profoundly engrains it upon your heart and mind. Don't worry, we won't actually do all this damage to your Bible because we are going to print out a copy of the text, beforehand. So, gather as many different colored markers, highlighters, and pens that you have, and let's get started.

Follow these steps to complete a *Messy Bible* study:

Step 1 Choose a short New Testament book to study

This method works best with complete books of the Bible.

Step 2 Type the Scripture triple spaced

Leave room for big margins on the side, without any verse number markings, chapter divisions, or paragraph separations. In the typing process, you will begin to view familiar books with new eyes. However if you want to cheat, you can copy and paste the Scripture from a website.

Step 3 Read the entire book

As you read the passage you are studying, look for the main theme. Try to follow the writer's train of thought.

Step 4 On the second reading your paper is alive with color

Read it again, this time marking themes, commands, key phrases, and so on. Let loose on marking it up because this is a print out, not your actual Bible.

Colors to Use When Marking Your Bible

- Use a <u>yellow highlighter</u> to mark verses to memorize.
- Use <u>blue circles</u> to mark repetitive words.
- Use <u>green double-underscores</u> to note the underlying theme.
- Use <u>red circles</u> to note warnings.
- Use <u>orange circles</u> to note references to our purpose in life.
- Use <u>purple boxes</u> to note descriptions of godly characteristics.

Symbols to Use When Marking Your Bible

O Circle the passages that you like.

? Question the verses that puzzle you.

X What you need to remove from your life.

> Arrow actions you want to take.

_ Underline actions you want to avoid.

= Place an equal sign next to commands you're already obeying in your life.

:) Place a smiley face over what makes you glad about God.

These marking methods are examples only. Feel free to use any colors, boxes, and arrows in whatever way works best for you. Draw figures, lightning bolts, anything that will help the passage come to life—this study is doodling with a purpose!

Step 5 Divide and organize the text

Decide where to insert paragraph breaks and place a black border around them to separate them from each other. This process will reveal the flow and relationship of ideas and principles.

Step 6 Read the book again and make notes in the margin

- Write any observations and/or questions in the margin.
- Write cross-references that come to mind.
- Use arrows to connect related ideas.
- Look up definitions of any confusing words.

Step 7 Use commentaries and reference books to research

Write any insights gained from these study tools in the margins. Look for answers to any questions you have previously written.

Step 8 Meditation and application

All this coloring and marking is ultimately for one reason—to bring you to your final question, which should be, "Father, how should I respond to what you've shown me?"

chapter

26

Modern Issues

The Bible contains wisdom for every life issue. While each situation may not be mentioned specifically in Scripture, principles exist that can be applied to every circumstance we face. For instance, we won't find the word "abortion" in the Bible, but in Psalm 139 we can read God's view on when life begins. We won't see the word "pornography" in the Bible, but we do see God's strong warnings to avoid lust, guard our eyes, and keep focused on godly pursuits. When it comes to problems, I cannot think of an area or issue of life that falls outside of God's wisdom. The Bible is full of His counsel—His Word provides every answer. From cover to cover, it reveals all we need to know in order to live godly lives. In Scripture, God has truly given us "all things that pertain to life and godliness" (2 Peter 1:3).

However, no perfect method exists for examining modern problems in light of biblical principles. It would be disingenuous to say otherwise. So, while not perfect, the following steps may prove helpful in bringing biblical solutions to some of life's modern situations.

Follow these steps to complete a *Modern Issues* Bible study:

Step 1 Pray for biblical wisdom
Ask God to guide your thinking, specifically that He would help you to differentiate between your own predetermined ideas and thoughts, and what the Bible teaches on the subject.

Step 2 Describe the problem in detail

Gather as much information as possible and examine the arguments on all sides of the case.

Step 3 Decide which biblical principles apply to the situation

You can use a good topical Bible such as *Naves Topical Bible*, or the *Thompson Chain Reference Bible* to research biblical topics related to the issue at hand. By searching synonyms, related phrases, and passages of Scripture that are relevant to your situation you will find godly direction. Consider carefully how the Scriptures you are searching can be applied to the problem you are dealing with today. In view of our modern lifestyle, determine which timeless biblical truths seem to fit your circumstance, and write those verses down.

Step 4 Check your interpretation of the verses researched

Always be sure that your application of biblical principles are not in conflict with other revealed Bible truths. Check the context in order to find clarity and to ensure that you are interpreting the verse accurately.

Step 5 Write your conclusion in a clear statement

Include verse references to back up your thoughts, and again, make sure that your statement lines up with biblical truth.

Step 6 Check your findings with other believers

It is always good to ask other believers for their thoughts on how you are interpreting a passage when the circumstances seem a little unclear. They may be able to suggest other applicable Scriptures that you haven't considered, or point out where you may have misused a passage or taken it out of context. If necessary, prayerfully edit your statement.

Step 7 Application

Ask the Lord for peace regarding the research you did on how to deal with this problem from a biblical perspective. Once you receive His peace, decide how you are going to apply what you have learned. However, if you don't sense His peace about your direction, prayerfully continue to do more research.

The next page has a sample of the Modern Issues Bible study method.

MODERN ISSUES

PROBLEM - Should we as Christians be concerned with the nation of Israel? What about our government? As some say, has Israel been replaced by the church?

WHICH VERSES APPLY
- Romans 11:1 - 'Has God cast off His people? Certainly not.'
- Ezekiel 37:22 - 'And I will make them one nation in all the land upon the mountains of Israel.'
- Romans 15:27 - 'For if the gentiles have been partakers of their spiritual things, their duty is also to minister to them in material things.'

CHECK INTERPRETATION - The context of these verses seem to point that I am applying them correctly here.

CONCLUSION - From these verses, I see that the creation of the modern state of Israel is a fullfillment of God's Word (Eze 37:22) and God has not forgotten about His covenant with them (Ro 11:1). We as a church and a nation should seek to bless the Jewish people and the land of Israel (Ro. 15:24, Ge 12:3).

[TEST MY FINDINGS] - I shared my conclusion with my pastor and he recommended I read Revelation 7 about the 144,000 Jews that are sealed in the end times. This supports my view that God is not done with Israel!

[APPLICATION] - I will begin to include the protection and blessing of Israel in my daily prayers starting today! Also, when I vote I will research the candidates support of Israel and use that to help make my decision.

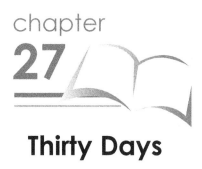

chapter
27

Thirty Days

Personally, I feel that this Bible study method is one of the most exciting—it is also one of the simplest! In short, it consists of choosing a New Testament book and reading it every day for a month. Reading the same book for thirty days will help you develop a deep understanding and familiarity with the text; you will begin to know it better than you ever have before, and will be able to identify and quickly locate passages within the book.

This study method is one that has become a part of my daily life. I usually do my devotions in the morning before the day's distractions begin. However, I was looking for a Bible study that would help me refocus my thoughts onto the Lord at the end of the day—this study is the perfect fit for me. It has not replaced my devotional life, but it has become a great way to bring my mind back to Him at the end of each day.

Too Much Time and Work

It may sound like a lot of effort to read a whole book of the Bible every day, but is it really? One night when I didn't feel like I had the strength or time to read the entire book of Ephesians, I decided to time myself in order to see how long it actually does take to read the book. I didn't do this to show off how fast I can read, (I'm an average reader) I did it to prove to myself that reading a few chapters of Scripture really doesn't take that much time. I did it to quiet my flesh! What I learned was that it only took me fifteen minutes to read the entire book at a normal pace. It's hard to justify not having fifteen minutes to devote to reading God's Word. So, if your flesh is saying it's too much to read a whole book of the Bible, maybe you should time yourself. I think you will be surprised to discover just how little time it really takes.

How to Do It

For the shorter epistles, reading the whole book in one sitting works great, but that doesn't mean you have to avoid studying the gospels or any of the longer epistles. If you choose to read a longer book, you can simply limit that month's reading to about seven chapters. The following month, continue reading the next seven chapters. It may take a few months to complete the book this way, but it will be worth the effort.

Does It Get Boring?

This method could become boring, but with a little discipline and variation, your time in God's Word will be fresh and exciting, every day. Below are a few hints that may help you overcome any feelings of repetition:

- Read the book aloud.
- Read it in different translations and try reading a paraphrase.
- Change locations—read at a coffee shop or while on a walk.
- Listen to the book using an MP3 audio version of the Bible.
- Watch a DVD version of the Bible, which allows you to hear the Scriptures while reading the words on the screen.
- Partner with someone else, and take turns reading the chapters.
- Print out the entire book and mark it up with colored markers.

Use your imagination. Some days I focus on finding my top ten favorite verses in the book. Then I'll choose a few of them to memorize that month. Other days I'll read commentaries on one chapter of the book along with my normal reading of the entire book. Sometimes I download messages from my favorite pastors who have taught verse-by-verse through that book, and I read along as I listen. What I've found is that when I get excited about being able to familiarize myself with a book of the Bible in just thirty days, I discover a number of creative ways to keep that time in the Word fresh.

Try It This Month

Why not give it a try for one month? I know if you do, you'll be hooked! It is an exciting way to study the Bible. Believe me—you'll be recommending this approach to people soon.

chapter

28

Vantage Point

One way to really change up your devotional life is to put yourself in the shoes of one of the characters in the story and write about it from that unique vantage point. Bible narratives take on new life when viewed in this way. For instance: Imagine what it must have been like to be standing on the shores of the Red Sea and watching as Moses parted them. Or, how about being one of the shepherds in the field outside of Bethlehem on the night that Jesus was born. What would it have been like to be one of those who were traveling on the Emmaus road when Jesus came along? Putting yourself into the story will add dimension to your understanding of God's Word because you will be engaging your mind, emotions, and imagination. However, I wouldn't recommend using this method of Bible study on a daily basis. This is most helpful when used only occasionally, to pull yourself out of a dry spell in your devotional life.

Follow these steps to begin a *Vantage Point* Bible study:

Step 1 Choose your story and read it in three translations

Before you reword the story see how others chose their words.

Step 2 Make a list of all the crucial facts about the story

What are the details that you just can't leave out? Make a timeline.

Step 3 Investigate the background

Learn something new about the characters, their situation, and customs of the time. You can find this information in study Bibles and commentaries.

Step 4 Pick your viewpoint character

Decide through whose eyes you are going to tell the story. It should be a person who was there, but not the main character.

Step 5 Write your story

Incorporate biblical facts and the new things you've learned from your background study. You can write your story as if it were a blog entry, a newspaper article, an email to a friend, or just a regular story. Just remember to stick to the facts. The point of this method is to understand a familiar Bible story in a new, more intimate way—not to rearrange the facts to say something other than what God intended.

Step 6 Application

Now that you have "experienced" this biblical story from this unique vantage point, spend a little time reflecting upon what God has shown you personally. How do you think you would have reacted if you lived during that time? What, if anything, needs to change in your life today because of this study? If you're feeling brave, share your story with others!

Can't Decide on a Story? Try One of These:

- The story of the flood, from the perspective of Noah's wife or one of his sons (Genesis 7-8).

- The Red Sea crossing, from the perspective of an Israelite child (Exodus 14).

- The destruction of city of Jericho, from the perspective of Rahab (Joshua 2 and 6).

- The story of David and Goliath, from the perspective of a Philistine (1 Samuel 17).

- The resurrection of Lazarus, from Lazarus' perspective (John 11).

- The Last Supper, from the perspective of Judas (Luke 22).

- Paul's conversion on the road to Damascus, from the perspective of one of Paul's fellow travelers (Acts 9:1-9).

The next page has a sample of the Vantage Point Bible study method.

VANTAGE POINT

[STORY] - Joseph (Genesis 39:20-41:14)
[PERSPECTIVE] - The prison guard

I've seen many prisoners, but never one such as this young lad, Joseph. His accusation is that of adultery with his master's wife, but I hardly believe it. Everything about this young man's character beams with honesty and integrity. In all my years, I have dealt with murmuring and complaints from so many prisoners, but never from Joseph. In fact, he has been a great help to me and I can trust him with matters here in the prison. And what's more, Joseph is kind, which is rare in a prison like ours. I asked Joseph once why he was so different. His answer shocked me as he began to talk about his God. I must admit, I was intrigued, for his God is not like our Egyptian gods. I'm not sure yet if I believe what he says, but I'll tell you this; if there really is a God like Joseph's, it is no wonder he lives as he does.

[APPLICATION] - I need to complain less about my job and be a better example of a Christian worker who serves God. (Colossians 3:23)

chapter

29

Skeptics Method

One of the most famous skeptics of all time was a man named Thomas. He was the apostle who doubted that Jesus had risen from the dead. Despite the claims of the other apostles, who saw the Lord and tried to convince him that Jesus was alive, Thomas refused to accept the truth. It wasn't until Jesus, Himself, showed Thomas the wounds in His hands and side that he finally believed (John 20:24-29).

We all have at least one doubting Thomas in our lives—a person who wants to see more evidence before believing our claims about Jesus. This Bible study method will help equip you to share the Scriptures with skeptics in a way that promotes communication and causes them to consider biblical truth.

Follow these steps to begin a *Skeptics Method* Bible study:

Step 1 Select a passage and read it as if this is the first time

As you read, remember, not everyone understands biblical words and concepts, such as sanctification and justification. Can you explain the passage in plain English? What would you say if you were sharing these truths with a skeptic? Note any concepts that may seem simple to you but will be foreign to others.

Step 2 Think about how this passage relates to unbelievers

What everyday situations and struggles does this passage address? What eternal truth is being taught? Can you think of an example that would help an unbeliever see how the wisdom of these Scriptures can apply to their circumstances, today.

Step 3 What possible objections might they have?

Put yourself in the mind of a skeptic and consider the kinds of questions they will pose? For instance: Will they wonder how miracles are possible? Will they have different opinions then the Bible offers?

Step 4 Consider how you would answer their objections

Do you have a good explanation for any issue they may raise? 1 Peter 3:15 encourages us to always have a good answer to defend our faith. If needed, research your answers using commentaries, apologetics resources, and by speaking with other mature Christians. Note any examples, outside of the Bible, that would demonstrate this truth.

Step 5 Prepare a brief testimony

If you have a related testimony of how following these Scriptures has benefitted you, share your story with them. It is helpful to show how practical the Bible is to our lives.

Step 6 Choose someone to share this with

Think of someone whose situation matches the ones you thought about in step two. Pray about the right way to encourage that person with these truths. It could be by sending a card that references the Scripture, calling and asking if you could pray with them about that situation, mailing them a Christian book with similar answers to their problems, or just casually bringing up in conversation that "you were just reading about the same thing in your Bible." God will honor your attempts to speak the truth in love. Choose a person and set a deadline for when you will share with them.

The next page has a sample of the Skeptics Method Bible study.

SKEPTICS METHOD

SCRIPTURE - Proverbs 15:3

CHRISTIAN TERMS - striving = arguing

RELATE TO UNBELIEVERS LIFE - This verse applies to anyone who gets in fights. If they would be willing to drop the issue and stop arguing the fight won't esculate.

POSSIBLE OBJECTIONS - How can there be honor in losing an arguement? Why should I let them win if I'm right? It seems weak.

MY ANSWER - You can still make your points calmly. It's better sometimes to lose a fight to keep a friend. There is no weakness in self-control. When arguements are allowed to esculate, it opens the door for unwanted pain (words you'll regret saying, and violence)

PERSONAL TESTIMONY - There was a time I really wanted to let someone have it, but I walked away while they were yelling. Later that night they called to apologize and we're still close friends.

HOW WILL I SHARE TRUTH - I will share this with my cousin with a temper over dinner tomorrow.

STUDYING SPECIFIC PASSAGES

Diverse Techniques for Studying
Certain Biblical Topics

These methods help believers discover and study many different themes and topics contained within the Scriptures. They add variety and depth to Bible study.

chapter

30

Royal Wisdom

The lives of biblical rulers (such as the kings of Judah and Israel) teach us the value of obedience to God. Most of the kings mentioned in the Bible were wicked kings. Some of them started out good, but ended badly. Only a few of them stayed strong in the Lord for their entire reign. As we read the stories of these leaders, we find many life lessons. The Bible documents the successes and failures of these kings to draw attention to the emotions, attitudes, thoughts, decisions, reactions, and relationships that can bring us closer to God, or lead us farther away from Him. Whether good or bad, their life stories can help us walk closer with Jesus, our King of kings.

Follow these steps to complete a *Royal Wisdom* Bible study:

Step 1 Choose a king to study

The life stories of the kings of Israel and Judah are found in 1 and 2 Kings and in 1 and 2 Chronicles, and are fun to read. They contain great narratives that are full of the exciting accounts surrounding the lives of Israel's kings. As you read these books make note of a few of the kings whose lives you would like to study in a little more detail. And remember, you can learn just as much from the bad kings and their mistakes, as you can from those who were good and godly rulers. (Be sure to read their stories in both Kings and Chronicles.)

Step 2 List every biographical observation, such as:

- Who was his father and which of his sons ruled after him?

- At what age did he begin ruling and when did his reign end?

- Which kingdom did he rule over: Judah or Israel?

- Review chapter twenty for more Bible character questions to ask.

Step 3 List the lessons learned from his life

- What were his biggest mistakes?

- What were his best decisions?

- How would you characterize his relationship with God?

- How did his reign as king end (good or bad)?

Step 4 Compare his life to yours

- In what ways are you similar to the king you have been studying?

- List a few character qualities (good and bad) that you have in common with him.

Step 5 Personal application

- Make a list of the attitudes and behaviors of the king that you would like to emulate, if any.

- List any attitudes and behaviors that you have in common with the king that should be cast off.

Step 6 Lock down the truth

- What is your response to what God is teaching you?

- Spend time in prayer asking the Lord to help you apply the lessons you've been learning. Be specific as you pray, mentioning the rulers name, their successes and failures, and your desire to either avoid or imitate the choices they made.

- Memorize one verse that was important to you from the story.

- For accountability, consider discussing this with a friend. Ask them to pray that you would grow in the character traits you desire to advance in.

The next page has a sample of the Royal Wisdom Bible study method.

ROYAL WISDOM

KING TO STUDY - Josiah

SCRIPTURE - 2 Kings 22-23 , 2 Chronicles 34-35

OBSERVATION
- Josiah, son of Amon, was 8 when he began his reign
- Josiah died in battle
- He ruled Judah
- He inspired reform in the nation

LESSONS TO LEARN
- Josiah was interested in doing things God's way (2 Kings 22:13)
- King Josiah was determined and focused on obeying God, so he made a covenant to follow the Lord (2 Kings 23:3)
- Josiah's relationship with God was strong (2 Kings 23:25)
- Josiah finished as a good king (2 Chronicles 35:26)

HOW DO I COMPARE
As I look at King Josiah, I am challenged in my own heart. I long to have more of the boldness and stability that he demonstrated in 2 Kings 23:3, and like him, I hope to end well.

APPLICATION

Qualities to emulate - humility, repentance, obedience. I want to be more like Josiah by issuing some non-negotiable reforms for my own heart. I'll search for areas that need change when I pray tonight (Psalm 139:23-24).

Qualities to cast off - legalism.
This issue was more with Josiah's kingdom than with himself. I have to guard my heart from just following a list of rules and make sure my end goal is to be loving God more.

LOCKING DOWN THE TRUTH

I'm going to memorize 2 Kings 22:13 this week.

chapter
31

Categorizing Proverbs

The thirty-one chapters in the book of Proverbs provide godly wisdom on almost every subject in life. The theme of Proverbs is found in Proverbs 1:7, "The fear of the Lord is the beginning of knowledge, but fools despise wisdom and instruction." This theme of the centrality of the knowledge of God runs throughout the entire book. Additionally, many other supporting themes exist in Proverbs that give us a complete picture of godly wisdom.

Many people choose to read one chapter of Proverbs a day. Since there are thirty-one chapters, they read "the chapter of the day" (i.e., chapter one on the first day of the month). Rarely does one chapter of Proverbs follow a single theme. The book is written in such a way that every few verses deal with a different issue. I've found that placing these verses into categories as I read helps me to get more out of the book of Proverbs. The acronym: **A LIFE FAILS,** will help you to remember the categories and also serves as a great reminder of the message of the book, because "a life fails" when it doesn't follow godly wisdom.

Follow these steps to complete a *Categorizing Proverbs* Bible study:

Step 1 Create your own book
Staple eleven pages of paper together into a small book. On the first page, create a book cover for your study (use your imagination). Next, at the top of each of the remaining ten pages write in bold one of the following category titles.

A - Abominations: What God Hates v. What God Loves

L - Lust v. Love

I - Injustice v. Justice

F - Folly v. Wisdom

E - Evil Tongue v. Good Tongue

F - False Security v. Real Security

A - Anger v. Joy

I - Immorality v. Morality

L - Laziness v. Diligence

S - Stinginess v. Generosity

<u>Note</u>: In every category a VICE is contrasted with its opposing VIRTUE.

Step 2 Read a chapter

Before beginning, spend time in prayer with the Author of the book of Proverbs. No, not Solomon—the Holy Spirit! He is the One who inspired Solomon to write this book. Next, read the chapter of Proverbs that corresponds to that day's date. This is a fun study to start at the beginning of the month, but any day of the month works just as well.

Step 3 Separate verses into categories

As you are reading, separate each proverb into a category. If many of the verses relate to the same category for that day, write one of the verses down and record the references for the rest. By the end of the month, you will have your own "topical version" of this book of wisdom.

Step 4 Application

Hopefully this method of study will help you think more deeply about how these Proverbs make us wiser. Ask God to show you how to apply this wisdom in your life and remember, "A LIFE FAILS" when godly advice is ignored. Visit http://www.LearnToStudyTheBible.com to compare your completed thirty-one day study with our index of themes and verse references.

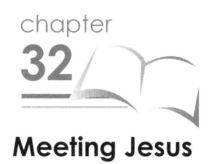

chapter

32

Meeting Jesus

W WJD (What Would Jesus Do?)—Let's find out!

Meeting with Jesus every day is the greatest privilege we have as Christians, but how do we meet with someone that we can't physically see? Grab a red-letter edition of the New Testament (a New Testament that has all of Jesus' words printed in red) and let's get started!

Follow these steps to complete a *Meeting Jesus* Bible study:

Step 1 Select a passage
Go through the gospels and select either an entire chapter or a single event in the life of Jesus. To get the full picture, check the other three gospels to see whether this story is recorded in them as well.

Step 2 Read the story for background information
Write down some basic information. Where is Jesus? Is He in a town, a region, a synagogue? Who is currently with Him?

Step 3 Read the story for context
Back up and read a few of the preceding paragraphs. Where was Jesus? What was He doing? Who was He interacting with? This will help you determine the context of the current situation. Do you think He is tired, thirsty, or hungry? Now read the next few paragraphs to see what Jesus

will be doing after this. Does knowing the context help your understanding of the passage you are currently studying?

Step 4 Summarize all that Jesus says

Briefly describe in your own words the main points of what Jesus is saying. Everything is in the Bible for a reason, and when things are left out of the Bible it's also for a reason. Can you think of anything you'd have said if you were in His sandals? Why do you think Jesus didn't say those things?

Step 5 Note the emotions and tone of Jesus

This step will help you relate to the humanity of Jesus. Take notice of every situation where Jesus shows compassion, anger, shock, sadness, joy, or any other emotion. Note any changes in His tone and why you think they occurred.

Step 6 Observe the way He responds to people

Does He answer their questions? Does He agree with their requests?

Step 7 Write what others are saying to, or about, Jesus

Are they asking questions, making observations, giving a warning, or praising Him?

Step 8 Record their impressions of Jesus

How do the people in the story seem to feel about Jesus? Are they amazed? Angered? Amused? Who do they think He is? Where do they think He gets His power? Often these impressions are clearly stated, but sometimes you may have to read between the lines.

Step 9 Write how people respond to Him

What did the people do after their encounter with Jesus? Did they believe and follow Him? Laugh at Him? Ask Him to leave? Plot to kill Him? Everyone who met Jesus responded to Him in some way. Did those in the account you read today respond correctly to Him?

Step 10 How have your impressions of Jesus changed?

What new thoughts about Jesus do you have since completing this study? Share those thoughts with Him in prayer!

Step 11 How will you respond to Jesus?

How did those you read about respond to Jesus? When you look at the inappropriate responses to the Son of God, ask yourself if you have ever responded to Him in the same way. You probably picked up some good responses that you want to emulate yourself. What changes in your life can you make to respond better to Jesus today?

The next page has a sample of the Meeting Jesus Bible study method.

MEETING JESUS

SCRIPTURE · John 2:1-12

BACKGROUND INFO

Jesus is in Cana of Galilee at a wedding.
With Him are wedding guests, servants, and
His disciples.

CONTEXT
· Before - The previous day Jesus had met
Nathanael and Nathanael learned Jesus
was the Son of God.
· After - Jesus went to Capernaum with His
family and disciples, then went to celebrate
Passover in Jerusalem.

SUMMARIZE JESUS' WORDS
· 2:4 - Jesus speaks to His mother, Mary, about
His hour having not yet come. Jesus talks
a lot about His "hour" in John's Gospel.
· 2:7-8 - Jesus gives instructions to the servants
regarding the water pots.

EMOTIONS AND TONE OF VOICE OF JESUS
In this story, Jesus seems very calm and
joyful. I imagine He was smiling as He gave
instructions to the servants because He
knew the miracle He was about to do.

JESUS' RESPONSE
Jesus' response to His mother's request was a little hard to understand, but He did what she asked Him to do.

WHAT OTHERS ARE SAYING ABOUT JESUS
Not much is said about Jesus in this passage but we see Mary's confidence in Him when she tells the servants "whatever He says, do it."

IMPRESSIONS OF JESUS
I am sure that the servants recognized it was the miraculous power of Christ that turned the water into wine and I bet they were impressed.

HOW DID PEOPLE RESPOND TO JESUS
The disciples, in seeing this miracle, believed in Him.

HOW HAS MY IMPRESSION CHANGED?
I am blessed to see Jesus providing for a young couple at their wedding. Jesus likes to see people happy.

HOW WILL I RESPOND?
I can take Mary's advice. Whatever Jesus says, do it! I'm going to bless a family at my church with a restaurant gift card so they can have a joyful feast too!

chapter

33

Twenty Jesus Questions

We can all think of questions we would like to ask Jesus if we had the opportunity, but did you know that He also wants to ask us a few questions? Jesus often asked questions of His followers as He taught them about His kingdom. It was His way of getting the people to think outside of the "religious box" of that day. Many of the religious traditions practiced by God's people at that time held the same weight and authority as the Word of God. This led to confusion because most of those traditions were man-made and did not accurately reveal God's heart. The questions Jesus asked of the people were meant to challenge them to come to a better knowledge of the truth about God and His heart for them. Today, we can study those questions that Jesus asked and learn more about God too. Todd D. Catteau has developed an interesting approach for Bible study based on Jesus' questions. He says that most of Jesus' questions fall under one of three categories.

#1 - QUESTIONS THAT Authenticate His Principles

Jesus often asked questions to prove that what He said made sense. For instance, in Matthew 6:25 Jesus made this significant statement, "Do not worry about your life." To validate this teaching, He followed it with a series of questions in verses 25-27, saying: "Is not life more than food and the body more than clothing?...Are you not of more value than [the birds of the air]? Which of you by worrying can add one cubit to his stature?"

When we correctly answer Jesus' questions we will also agree with His original premise that worrying is pointless. Other examples of some of the validating questions Jesus asked are found in Luke 6:27-34 and 9:23-25.

#2 - QUESTIONS THAT Confront False Views

Jesus lived at a time when false ideas about God were flourishing—much like today. His questions often challenged the false teaching that His people blindly adhered to. For instance, in Luke 13:1-2, Jesus challenged the Jews in their accepted belief that suffering was a direct result of sin. Following a report of a tragedy involving the death of some Galileans, Jesus contested their false assumptions by asking, "Do you suppose that these Galileans were worse sinners than all other Galileans, because they suffered such things?" His question forced His followers to consider their view. Other examples can be found in Matthew 15:1-3 and 16:13-15. Examining Jesus' questions will help us to see where our view of what God is doing today may also be wrong.

#3 - QUESTIONS THAT Enlarge Our Faith

Jesus often prefaced miracles with questions. For instance, in John 5:6 Jesus asked the sick man by the pool of Bethesda, "Do you want to be made well?" On the surface that may seem like a preposterous thing to ask—of course the man wants to be well. So why did Jesus ask the question? Perhaps it was to help the man see that he was putting his faith in the wrong thing. Jesus asked questions such as these to help people put their faith in Him. He also asked faith-building questions following episodes that demonstrated a lack of faith. For example, in Matthew 14:31, Jesus rescued Peter from his attempt to walk on water and then asked him, "Why did you doubt?" Surely, that simple question rang in Peter's ears for the rest of his life. It probably also helped him to remember not to doubt Jesus when faced with difficult situations.

How can we work these questions into a Bible study? These steps will help you organize and chart your thoughts.

Step 1 Find a question

Search the gospels to find a question that Jesus asked that you would like to study. Otherwise, you can use one of the twenty questions at the end of this chapter to get started.

Step 2 Identify the type of question it is

Determine whether the question you selected was meant to authenticate, confront, or build faith. It is possible that it could fit in more than one category; however, you will need to choose only one before moving forward.

Step 3 Complete the appropriate steps in this chart

AUTHENTICATING QUESTIONS	CONFRONTING QUESTIONS	FAITH QUESTIONS
Write the question:	Write the question:	Write the question:
Step 1 - Find the statement being authenticated:	Step 1 - Identify the false teaching being confronted:	Step 1 - Determine the context of the question:
Step 2 - List potential objections to the statement:	Step 2 - Discuss the origins of these false ideas:	Step 2 - Determine the question's significance:
Step 3 - Describe how the objections are resolved:	Step 3 - Arrive at a clearer understanding of the truth:	Step 3 - Ask how the question deepens faith:

Step 4 End in prayer

Prayer is an integral part of this study. It will help you see the answers that Jesus' questions were intended to reveal, and have an impact upon your life. Depending on which type of question you are studying, the following suggestions may help you to begin praying more specifically.

1. **Authenticating Questions**: Pray that God will enable you to see the spiritual rationale behind Jesus' teachings, more clearly.

2. **Confronting Questions:** Ask God to help you understand Him based solely on the truth of Scripture: ask Him to help you let go

of any false assumptions or teachings that you have believed about Him in the past.

   3. Faith Questions: Ask God to help you continue to grow in your faith in Him.

Twenty Questions from Jesus to Get You Started

Before beginning your study, be sure to classify each of these questions as an authenticating, confronting, or faith question.

 1. Why do you look at the speck in your brother's eye? (Matthew 7:3)

 2. What man is there among you who, if his son asks for bread, will give him a stone? (Matthew 7:9)

 3. Who is My mother and who are My brothers? (Matthew 12:48)

 4. How long shall I bear with you? (Matthew 17:17)

 5. Which is greater, the gold or the temple? (Matthew 23:17)

 6. How many loaves do you have? (Mark 8:5)

 7. Who do you say that I am? (Mark 8:29)

 8. Why do you call Me good? (Mark 10:18)

 9. Why do you trouble her? (Mark 14:6)

10. Why have You forsaken Me? (Mark 15:34)

11. If you love those who love you, what credit is that? (Luke 6:32)

12. Why do you call me, 'Lord, Lord,' and not do the things which I say? (Luke 6:46)

13. Were there not ten cleansed? (Luke 17:17)

14. What do you want Me to do for you? (Luke 18:41)

15. Ought not the Christ to have suffered these things? (Luke 24:26)

16. Are you the teacher of Israel, and do not know? (John 3:10)

17. Do you also want to go away? (John 6:67)

18. Woman, where are those accusers of yours? (John 8:10)

19. Are there not twelve hours in the day? (John 11:9)

20. Shall I not drink the cup which My Father has given? (John 18:11)

The next page has a sample of the Twenty Jesus Questions Bible study.

20 JESUS QUESTIONS

AUTHENTICATING QUESTIONS	CONFRONTING QUESTIONS
"Who is my mother, and who are my brothers?" (Matthew 12:48)	"Which is greater, the gold or the temple?" (Matthew 23:17)
1-Authenticated Statement: Whoever does the will of my Father in heaven is my sister, brother, mother.	1-Identify the False: That outward appearance is more important than inner heart.
2-Potential Objections: Only related if it is biologically.	2-Reasons for False Ideas: It is much easier to make people think everything is fine on the outside
3-Objections Resolved: Jesus is sharing that in His spiritual family, obedience is important	3-Clearer Understanding: It is more important that our hearts are right before God then just our actions

FAITH
QUESTIONS
"What do you want me
to do for you?
(Luke 18:41)

1-Context of Question:
Jesus is speaking to
a blind man.

2-Significance:
Jesus was giving the
man a chance to voice
his request to God.

3-Deepened Faith:
May the Lord give me
faith to believe on
Him for the impossible

chapter
34

The Commands of Jesus

We all pray for God's direction in life, especially when we desire to know His will for an important decision we need to make. In most cases, we find ourselves having to choose between one good option and another. It would be easy if one of our choices was obviously wrong, but it can get frustrating when we are not sensing God's clear guidance in either direction. When I'm in one of those situations I find it helpful to go back to the basics—what are the things that I already know God has called me to do? Staying focused on what I do know, helps me to wait for His answers on those things that I'm not sure of yet.

The Bible gives us a wealth of clear commands from God that brings strength, direction, and satisfaction into our lives. In fact, the New Testament is emphatic about the importance of knowing and heeding Christ's Word. Obeying Jesus proves that we love Him (John 14:15, 21-24). It is exciting when we can know and obey the expressed will of God in our lives.

Follow these steps to complete a *Commands of Jesus* Bible study:

Step 1 Choosing a command

Jesus gave us specific and clear commands in Scripture. Any verse that states authoritatively what must or must not be done, thought, said, or allowed in the life of a believer are meant to be obeyed. If you have a copy of the Bible that has the Words of Jesus in red letters use that to begin searching the gospels to find His commands. Pick one that you would like to study further.

Step 2 Studying the command

First, find the context by reading the verses surrounding the one that contains the command. Then answer these questions:

- What is the immediate context of the command?
- What topic does the command address?
- How did the command challenge the original audience?
- What is the consequence of breaking this command?
- What are the eternal benefits of keeping this command?
- What questions do I have about it? Does it make sense to me?
- What other related passages do the cross-references point to?
- Do I see this command being lived out in the Old Testament?
- What timeless principle(s) does this command embody?
- What is the command telling me, and how should I apply it?

Charting the answers to these questions will help you organize your thoughts and store them in an easily retrievable format.

Step 3 Obeying the command

What is your personal response to Christ's command in this verse? Prayerfully consider any changes that you may need to make in order to ensure that you will obey His Word. If necessary, confess and repent of any sin, and ask the Holy Spirit to give you the power to surrender your will fully in order to follow Jesus faithfully.

Develop a specific action plan and be determined to obey God no matter what. Since we tend to paint ourselves in the best light, you might also want to ask someone you trust such as a family member, friend, neighbor, or coworker, to honestly evaluate your behavior and obedience to God's revealed will, in this area.

The next page has a sample of The Commands of Jesus Bible study method.

THE COMMANDS OF JESUS

SCRIPTURE - Matthew 6:34

COMMAND - "Therefore, do not worry about tomorrow..."

CONTEXT - Jesus is speaking to His disciples in the Sermon on the Mount.

TOPIC - This command has to do with worrying as to whether or not the Lord will provide for our basic needs.

CHALLENGE TO ORIGINAL AUDIENCE
They had to decide if they were going to trust in God or in themselves.

CONSEQUENCES OF BREAKING COMMAND
I will overload my day with worry and accomplish little for Christ.

ETERNAL BENEFITS OF KEEPING COMMAND
My faith in God will grow.

QUESTIONS ABOUT COMMAND
"Sufficient for the day is its own trouble" kind of makes it seem like worrying about today is alright.

RELATED PASSAGES
- James 4:13-17
- Proverbs 3:5-6
- Jeremiah 29:11
- Philippians 4:6-7

OT EXAMPLE OF COMMAND
The widow in 1 Kings 17:8-16 who made food for Elijah before she made it for herself or her son. It worked out great for her! God provided until the drought ended.

TIMELESS PRINCIPLE
God is our provider, always has been and always will be.

PERSONAL APPLICATION
Next time I find myself worrying, I'm going to write my worries out as a prayer to the Lord and then leave them for Him to take care of.

chapter

35

Truly, Truly

A ll of the words that Jesus spoke were truth; as He told Pilate, He came into this world to "bear witness to the truth" (John 18:37). Yet, at times, when He wanted to place special emphasis upon the importance of what He was about to say, He used a phrase to draw attention to that fact. Depending upon which version of the Bible you have, the phrase Jesus used at those times, was:

- Most assuredly (NKJV)
- I tell you the truth (NIV)
- Amen, amen, or verily, verily (KJV)
- Truly, truly (NASB and ESV)

Essentially, Jesus was urging His followers to take note of the importance of understanding the truth that He was about to tell them. He could not say it any clearer or with any greater emphasis—He was speaking about a truth that was an absolute necessity.

The KJV translates this phrase as, **amen, amen**. When God says "amen" He is saying, "it is and shall be so" and when men respond back by saying "amen" they are agreeing, "so let it be." In the NKJV of John 3:3, we read, "Jesus answered and said to him, '**Most assuredly**, I say to you, unless one is born again, he cannot see the kingdom of God.'" The phrase, "most assuredly" is used twenty-five times in the gospel of John alone, and reminds us that the words Jesus spoke about salvation are certain and true.

What we believe to be true affects every decision we make, so knowing and responding to God's truth is critical. The truth frees and empowers us to live a life that pleases the Lord. As Jesus said, "You shall know the truth, and the truth shall make you free" (John 8:32). By studying the statements that Jesus strongly emphasized throughout the gospels, we will be encouraging ourselves in God's certain truth in an uncertain world.

The following steps will help you complete a *Truly, Truly* Bible study:

Step 1 Identify the truth Jesus speaks

Choose one of the "most assuredly" statements from the list below and pinpoint the truth that Jesus' words reveal. Write down this truth keeping the context of His statement in mind by reading the surrounding verses.

The "Most Assuredly" Sayings of Jesus in the Gospel of John:

John 1:51; 3:3; 3:11; 5:19; 5:24; 5:25; 6:26; 6:32; 6:47; 6:53; 8:34; 8:51;8:58; 10:1; 10:7;12:24; 13:16; 13:20; 13:21; 13:38; 14:12; 16:20; 16:23; 21:18.

Step 2 Observe the timeless principle

What did this truth mean to those to whom it was first addressed? Review the verse in context to determine the timeless principle that we can apply from its meaning today.

Step 3 Detect the world's lie

Almost every statement of truth that Jesus made counters a lie that the Devil would like us to believe. As you meditate on the truth, the subtle lies of the enemy will become more obvious and you will be less likely to be tripped up by his schemes. Completing this step will help you recognize temptation more quickly and be prepared to overcome with the truth.

Step 4 How can you obey?

It takes more than just knowing the truth—we need to obey it too. Once you know what God is saying, begin personally applying it in your life. In light of what you have learned, what changes do you need to make?

The next page has a sample of the Truly, Truly Bible study method.

TRULY, TRULY

SCRIPTURE	TIMELESS PRINCIPLE
John 6:26 - "Most assuredly, I say to you, you seek Me, not because you saw the signs, but because you ate the loaves and were filled."	God knows our hearts and how our motives for following people can be selfish.
John 8:34 - "Most assuredly, I say to you, whoever commits sin is a slave of sin.	There is no little sin. Sin entangles you in its web. You can't handle it or control it. It controls you.

WORLD'S LIE	HOW TO OBEY
Follow whoever gives you what you want. When they stop providing then go follow someone else who will provide.	I need to trust Jesus at all times, even when He does not answer my prayers how I want Him to. I have to remind myself to seek Him for WHO He is, not WHAT He can give me.
You are strong enough and smart enough to get as close to sin as you want. It's no big deal, you can always stop. Just try it once.	I need accountability partners to ask me direct questions about how close I get to sin. I need to treat all sin as horrible and deadly and get away from it ASAP!

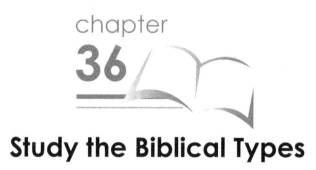

chapter
36

Study the Biblical Types

The Old and New Testaments fit together in perfect unity to reveal God's loving redemption of fallen man. The direct statements of God's grace and love towards us through Christ that we read about in the New Testament are portrayed more subtly in the typology of the Old. A type is a picture, representation, or symbol of something yet to come. The types contained in the Old Testament are divinely purposed and were placed in the text in order to foreshadow a New Testament spiritual reality that would one day be fulfilled in Jesus. Finding these precious truths buried away in what seems like a very dry and obscure portion of the Bible, is exciting!

Unfortunately, the study of biblical types has been greatly abused and over-done by some, but that is no reason to neglect them all together. All you need to do is guard yourself against any teaching that is too far-fetched. Anyone blessed with an imagination can easily get carried away with this kind of study and begin seeing types everywhere. A general rule of thumb when it comes to biblical types is to be able to point to an unmistakable passage of Scripture to confirm that the truth being typified is definitely taught. Ask the Holy Spirit to guide you in truth before you begin. To help you develop this sense of discernment, begin by familiarizing yourself with some simple and unmistakable types, like the ones in the first step.

The following steps will help you complete a *Biblical Types* Bible study:

Step 1 Choose a type and describe the truth it typifies

The following list from William MacDonald's *Enjoy Your Bible* is a great place to start when studying types. However, no type is perfect, especially in the case of types of our Lord.

- Joseph: Although he is never said to be a type of the Lord Jesus, according to authors Ada Habershon and Arthur Pink, over one hundred similarities can be made between his life and Christ's (Genesis 37-50).

- Noah's Ark: The ark's immersion in the waters of judgment pictures Christ's baptism unto death at Calvary. Just as those in the ark are saved, so those in Christ are saved (1 Peter 3:18-22).

- Melchidezek: "You [Christ] are a priest forever according to the order of Melchizedek" (Hebrews 7:17).

- Moses: Moses said, "The Lord your God will raise up for you a Prophet like me from your midst" (Deuteronomy 18:15).

- Passover: "Christ, our Passover, was sacrificed for us" (1 Corinthians 5:7).

- The High Priest: "We have such a High Priest [in the Lord Jesus]" (Hebrews 8:1).

- The Veil of the Tabernacle: "through the veil, that is, His flesh" (Hebrews 10:20b).

- The Tabernacle: "And the Word became flesh and dwelt [literally, tabernacled or 'pitched His tent'] among us" (John 1:14).

- The Manna: Jesus said, "I am the living bread which came down from heaven" (John 6:51).

- The Rock: "For they drank of that spiritual Rock that followed them, and that Rock was Christ" (1 Corinthians 10:4b).

- The Serpent: "And as Moses lifted up the serpent in the wilderness, even so must the Son of Man be lifted up" (John 3:14).

Step 2 Research all Scripture

To keep the thought in context, look up all the Scripture references contained in the marginal references of your Bible, or in a topical index. If the New Testament speaks about the parallel then the type is without doubt, however we must be careful when identifying something as a type if we cannot find a New Testament Scripture as confirmation.

Step 3 Study the name of this possible type

Carefully study the meaning of the names of persons and places mentioned. Bible names often have very deep and far-reaching suggestiveness. For instance: Bethlehem, the name of the town where Jesus, our Bread of Life, was born, literally means "house of bread."

Step 4 Study included symbols of the type

Consider the possible interpretation of symbols within a type. For example, since the high priest is a type of Christ, then what may his linen garments symbolize about Jesus' ministry as our High Priest (Exodus 28:39)?

Step 5 Study the thing of which it is a type

First, we study the person, place, event, or thing and then we study that for which it is a type. In a way, types are like prophecies. They give an advance view of something that is to come in God's unfolding plan. Like prophecy, some types have already been fulfilled, while others have not yet come to pass.

Step 6 Make a chart of similarities

How is the possible type, and what it typifies, connected? Most of the time there is only one central point in the comparison, but secondary details can be present at times. How does this picture or type help you understand God's truth better? Share your list with another solid believer. This will give God a chance to show you through this person if any possible errors exist in your thinking.

Step 7 Make a list of differences

To keep your mind from wandering and getting too fanciful it is helpful to remind yourself of some ways that this type probably doesn't work perfectly. This doesn't mean that you can't enjoy your previous connections it simply helps keep you on the narrow path of truth.

Step 8 Personal application

Now that you have a clearer picture of a Bible truth from your study of this type, how will it affect the way you are living for the Lord? Did an area of your life that needs to change stand out to you? How can your life better typify God's truth?

The next page has a sample of the Biblical Types Bible study method.

STUDY THE TYPES

TYPE - The rock in the wilderness

EXPLANATION
As God's people wandered through the desert, they would no doubt need miraculous provision to survive. One need they had was water, since humans cannot survive without water, especially in a hot desert.

Simply and clearly, the rock is a type of Christ, for 1 Corinthians 10:4 says so.

Now the type is twofold. In Exodus 17, Moses was told to strike the rock and water would flow. In Numbers 20, he was simply told to speak to the rock. The type of Christ is clear. Jesus died once for sin, thus giving life in His name. He is not continually crucified, as we now only need to speak to Him and He graciously gives living water.

SCRIPTURES
• OT - Exodus 17:1-7, Numbers 20:1-13
• NT - 1 Corinthians 10:4

STUDY THE NAME - Christ and Rock
• Christ = Strong's #5547 - Christos - annointed, the Messiah, the Son of God

• Rock = Strong's #4073 – Petra – a rock, large stone, metaphor – a man like a rock, by reason of his firmness and strength of soul

INCLUDED SYMBOLS
• staff that struck rock may symbolize cross?
• Moses may symbolize the Father striking His Son?

STUDY THE THING OF WHICH IT'S A TYPE
• Jesus at the well, giving water (John 4)
• Jesus on the cross, being struck (John 19)

SIMILARITIES
• Rock's strength = Christ's strength
• Rock struck by staff = Christ struck by God
• Water from rock = water from Christ's side?
• Water from rock = Living water from Jesus

DIFFERENCES
• Rock struck twice = Jesus struck only once

APPLICATION
I will speak to Jesus today in prayer to receive all that I need. (Hebrews 4:16).

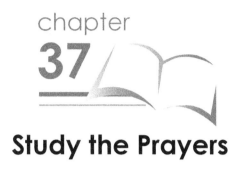

chapter

37

Study the Prayers

Today's high-speed Internet access makes it possible for us to stay in touch with each other literally around the clock. Yet, despite our technological advances, no one will ever be more accessible to us than Jesus—He is the originator of "24/7." We will never be able to come up with anything more awe-inspiring than the fact that at anytime we desire, we can speak directly to the One who created the universe. Sadly, however, many of us will spend more time talking on our cell phones than we will spend speaking to the Lord today, in prayer.

The more time they spent with Jesus, the more the disciples realized that He received His sustenance from periods of private prayer. That is why, of all the things they could have asked Him to teach them—i.e., how to heal the blind, raise the dead, multiply food, teach with authority, etc.—what those closest to Jesus wanted to learn from Him was how to pray. What we know today, as *The Lord's Prayer,* was His response to their request. However, in addition to the model He gave them in that prayer, the Bible contains over 500 other references to prayer, approximately 100 of which are actual recorded prayers. We will find a lot of wisdom and joy in studying both the doctrine of prayer, and the content of the many diverse prayers found in the Scriptures.

The following steps will help you begin to *Study the Prayers* in the Bible:

Step 1 Journal details about your current prayer time

- How often do you pray: daily/weekly? How much time do you spend in prayer?
- Do you pray "big" prayers? Small ones? Both?
- Do you keep a prayer journal to record your requests and answers?
- What is the most exciting answer you've ever received in prayer?
- What do you think is the biggest change you need to make in your prayer time?
- What benefits do you believe making those changes will bring?

Step 2 Choose a prayer to study

A suggested list of biblical prayers is provided at the end of this chapter to help you get started.

Step 3 Read the prayer

Read the prayer at least five times to familiarize yourself with its content.

Step 4 Outline the facts of the prayer

Take note of the way the prayer is structured and create an outline based upon what you find. Be sure to include verse references for each of the major and minor points. What elements does the prayer contain? (i.e., adoration, worship, thanksgiving, confession, intercession, or petition.)

Step 5 Study the prayer

On a separate piece of paper, answer the following questions:

1. Is the person praying a believer?
2. What circumstance led to the prayer? (i.e., knowledge of guilt, thankfulness, the need for guidance, healing, food, etc.)
3. What are the physical aspects surrounding the prayer? (i.e., time of day, public or private, on knees or standing, etc.)
4. What words are used to indicate that they are praying?
5. To whom is the prayer being directed?
6. Who is the main subject of the prayer?

7. What is the relation of the prayer to the <u>promises</u> found in the Word of God? Were any specific promises of God answered? Did the one who prayed have a right to expect an answer in light of the biblical promises?

8. Was the prayer <u>answered,</u> and if so, how and when? Under what circumstances was it answered?

9. What was the result of the prayer? What <u>effect</u> did it have on the one who offered it? On others? On those who heard it?

10. What has studying this prayer taught you <u>personally</u>?

Step 6 Pray the prayer!

Ask God to help you incorporate the lessons you have learned about prayer into your own personal prayer life. This may not work with every prayer recorded in the Bible, however, with a little rewording you should be able to fit most of them into your situation and be able to start praying God's Word back to Him. Close by spending time in prayer.

List of Prayers to Study

The following is a partial list of the prayers found in the Bible. The Old Testament contains approximately eighty-three prayers, while the New Testament has forty-nine.

Old Testament Prayers

- <u>Aaron and the priests</u> — Numbers 6:22-26, blessing for Israel
- <u>Abraham</u> — Genesis 15:2, for a son
- <u>Abraham</u> — Genesis 17:18, for Ishmael's acceptance
- <u>Abraham's servant</u> — Genesis 24:12, success in his mission
- <u>Asa II</u> — 2 Chronicles 14:11, when entering battle
- <u>Daniel</u> — Daniel 9:4-19, for restoration
- <u>David</u> — Psalm 51, for restoration
- <u>David</u> — 1 Chronicles 29:10-15, thanksgiving
- <u>Elijah</u> — 1 Kings 17:20, for restoration of life
- <u>Elijah</u> — 1 Kings 18:36-37, for vindication
- <u>Elijah</u> — 1 Kings 19:4, for release from life

- Ezekiel — Ezekiel 9:8, intercession for the people
- Ezra — Ezra 9:5-15, confession for the people
- Habakkuk — Habakkuk 2:1-20, for revival
- Hannah — 1 Samuel 1:11, for a son
- Hezekiah — 2 Kings 19:15-19, for protection
- Israel — Deuteronomy 21:6-8, for forgiveness
- Jabez — 1 Chronicles 4:10, for divine blessing
- Jacob — Genesis 32:9, for deliverance
- Jeremiah — Jeremiah 14:7-9, for salvation
- Jonah — Jonah 2:2, for deliverance
- Jeremiah —Jeremiah 15:15-18, for comfort
- Joshua — Joshua 7:7-9, cry of distress
- Moses — Exodus 32:11-14, for forgiveness
- Moses — Numbers 27:15-17, for a successor
- Nehemiah — Nehemiah 4:4-5, for protection
- Samson — Judges 16:28, for avenging
- Solomon — 1 Kings 3:5-9, for wisdom to govern
- Solomon — 1 Kings 8:22-53, dedication of the temple

New Testament Prayers

- Jesus — Luke 22:39-46, for courage
- Jesus — Luke 23:34, for forgiveness
- Jesus — Luke 23:46, for safekeeping
- Disciples — Matthew 6:9-15, the divinely given prayer pattern
- Disciples — Acts 4:23-31, for boldness
- Paul — Romans 1:9-12, for opportunity
- Paul — Ephesians 1:16-23, for knowledge and prayer
- Paul — Philippians 1:8-11, for maturity
- Paul — Colossians 1:9-14, for fruitfulness

The next page has a sample of the Study the Prayers Bible study method.

STUDY THE PRAYERS

PRAYER STUDIED – Acts 4:23-31

OUTLINE
- Praise (Acts 4:24-28)
- Petition (Acts 4:29-30)

WHO – Those praying are the disciples.

CIRCUMSTANCES – They have just been released from the Sanhedrin's custody.

PHYSICAL ASPECTS – Raising of voice, with one accord.

WORD USED – 'Raised their voice to God.'

TO WHOM – 'Lord... one who made heaven and earth and sea.'

MAIN SUBJECT – Prayer for boldness to continue speaking the word of God.

PROMISE – In prayer, they quote Psalm 2, thus they are praying in accordance with the word of God.

ANSWERED - Their prayer was answered!
A couple of things happened, the place was
shaken, they were filled with the Holy
Spirit, and, as requested, they spoke the
word of God with boldness.

EFFECT - They spoke with boldness, and
people got saved!

LESSON - Always pray in accordance
with the Word. God loves to answer
prayer according to His will.

chapter
38

Study the Miracles

Miracles are extraordinary events and are considered the handiwork of God. Even though they occur within our physical world, true miracles defy natural explanation. Miracles were one of the authenticating proofs that validated Jesus' divinity and revealed to those who knew the ancient prophecies that He was the long-awaited Messiah (John 5:36; 10:25, 38). Studying the miraculous events that occur in the Bible yields great truths.

In the New Testament four Greek words are used to designate miracles: (1) Semeion, a "sign," i.e., an evidence of a divine commission; the seal of a higher power (Matthew 12:38, 39; Mark 8:11). (2) Terata, "wonders;" wonder-causing events; portents; producing astonishment in the beholder (Acts 2:19). (3) Dunameis, "mighty works;" works of superhuman power (Acts 2:22); of a new and higher power. (4) Erga, "works;" the works of Him who is "wonderful in working" (John 5:20).

The following steps will help you *Study the Miracles* of the Bible:

Step 1 Choose a miracle to study and read it
A list of Bible miracles is provided at the end of this chapter to help get you started.

Step 2 Outline the miracle (make a timeline)
Create an outline of the miracle from the Bible's account.

Step 3 Study the miracle

Ask the following questions about this amazing work of God:

1. What does it <u>evidence</u> about the person who performed it?
2. What does the miracle reveal about the <u>nature of God</u>?
3. What does the miracle reveal about the <u>work of God</u> on earth? (What prompted Him to work in this unusual manner?)
4. What command or prayer <u>brought forth</u> the miracle?
5. What would <u>those who watched</u> have learned from this?
6. In the light of the total impact of Scripture, <u>why</u> do you think this miracle was recorded? (See John 20:30-31)

Step 4 Construct a chart

As shown on the sample, create a chart with the following information, listed in parallel columns:

- <u>Miracle</u>: Write a descriptive title and list the verse references.
- <u>Realm</u>: i.e., Nature (weather), Spiritual (demons), Physical (health).
- <u>Occasion</u>: What need prompted this miracle?
- <u>People</u>: Name everyone involved in this miracle.
- <u>Means</u>: Was the miracle performed through a touch, or a word?
- <u>Results</u>: Record what happened because of this miracle.
- <u>Reactions</u>: Write how the crowd responded afterwards.

When two or more miracles are recorded in a single passage, or when you want to compare a number of miracles that took place in one book of the Bible, record all the factors surrounding the miracles on the same chart and then draw your conclusions.

Step 5 Application

Explain the effect that studying this miracle has had on your daily walk with the Lord? Write any personal application that you are planning to make because of this study.

Partial List of Old Testament Miracles:

- Creation of the universe (Genesis 1-2)
- The flood (Genesis 7, 8)
- Confusion of languages (tongues) at Babel (Genesis 11:1-9)
- Destruction of Sodom and Gomorrah (Genesis 19:24)
- Birth of Isaac at Gerar (Genesis 21:1)
- The burning bush not consumed (Exodus 3:3)
- Aaron's rod changed into a serpent (Exodus 7:10-12)
- The ten plagues of Egypt (Exodus 7:20-12:30)
- Red Sea divided (Exodus 14:21-31)
- Waters of Marah sweetened (Exodus 15:23-25)
- Manna sent daily, except on Sabbath (Exodus 16:14-35)
- Water from the rock at Rephidim (Exodus 17:5-7)
- The earth opens and swallows up Korah (Numbers 16:31-34)
- Fire at Kadesh (Numbers 16:35-45)
- Plague at Kadesh (Numbers 16:46-50)
- Aaron's rod budding at Kadesh (Numbers 17:8)
- Water from the rock, struck twice by Moses (Numbers 20:7-11)
- The bronze serpent in the Desert of Zin (Numbers 21:8, 9)
- Balaam's donkey speaks (Numbers 22:21-35)
- The Jordan divided, so that Israel passed over (Joshua 3:14-17)
- The walls of Jericho fall down (Joshua 6:6-20)
- The sun and moon stayed (Joshua 10:12-14)
- Hailstorm (Joshua 10:12-14)
- Dagon falls twice before the ark (1 Samuel 5:1-12)
- Thunderstorm causes a panic to Philistines (1 Samuel 7:10-12)
- Jeroboam's hand withered (1 Kings 13:4)
- Widow of Zarephath's meal and oil increased (1 Kings 17:14-16)
- Sennacherib's army destroyed, Jerusalem (2 Kings 19:35)

Partial List of New Testament Miracles:

- Piece of money in the fish's mouth (Matthew 17:24-27)
- The deaf and dumb man (Mark 7:31-37)
- Jesus passes unseen through the crowd (Luke 4:28-30)
- The miraculous net of fish (Luke 5:4-11)
- The raising of the widow's son at Nain (Luke 7:11-18)
- The woman with the spirit of infirmity (Luke 13:11-17)
- The ten lepers (Luke 17:11-19)
- The healing of Malchus (Luke 22:50-51)
- Water made wine (John 2:1-11)
- Cure of nobleman's son, Capernaum (John 4:46-54)
- Paralyzed man at Bethsaida cured (John 5:1-9)
- Man born blind cured (John 9:1-7)
- Lazarus raised from the dead (John 11:38-44)
- Net of fish (John 21:1-14)
- Syrophoenician woman's daughter cured (Matthew 15:28)
- Four thousand fed (Matthew 15:32-39; Mark 8:1-8)
- Centurion's servant healed (Matthew 8:5-13; Luke 7:-101)
- Blind and dumb demoniac cured (Matthew 12:22; Luke 11:14)
- Peter's wife's mother cured (Matthew 8:14-15; Mark 1:30-31)
- The storm stilled (Matthew 8:23-27; Mark 4:37-39)
- Demon Possessed of Gadara cured (Matthew 8:28-32)
- Leper healed (Matthew 8:2-3; Mark 1:40-42; Luke 5:12-13)
- Jairus's daughter raised (Matthew 9:22-25; Mark 5:23)
- Woman's issue of blood cured (Matthew 9:20-22; Mark 5:25-34)
- Man's withered hand cured (Matthew 12:10-13; Mark 3:1-5)
- Two blind men cured (Matthew 20:29-34; Mark 10:46-52)

The next page has a sample of the Studying the Miracles Bible study.

STUDY THE MIRACLES

MIRACLE 1 - Raising of Lazarus (John 11:1-44)

OUTLINE

I. Lazarus Dies
   a) Mary and Martha send for Jesus (v.1-3)
   b) Jesus purposefully delays (v.4-6)
   c) Jesus instructs and corrects disciples (v.7-16)

II. Jesus Arrives in Bethany
   a) Lazarus already dead four days (v.17)
   b) Martha runs to meet Jesus (v.18-20)
   c) Martha believes in Jesus (v.21-27)

III. Jesus Consoles Mary
   a) Mary runs to Jesus (v.28-31)
   b) Mary cries with Jesus (v.32)
   c) Jesus cries with Mary (v.33-36)

IV. Lazarus Raised from the Dead
   a) Jesus goes to the tomb (v.38-39)
   b) Jesus asks Mary to have faith (v.40)
   c) Jesus prays outloud for crowd (v.41-42)
   d) Jesus calls for Lazarus (v.43)
   e) Lazarus lives again (v.44)

THE HUMAN WHO PERFORMED IT
Jesus performed this miracle and must have been given supernatural powers by God.

THE NATURE OF GOD
It shows us that God has compassion, has power over death, and gives life.

THE WORK OF GOD ON EARTH
Anything asked in faith can be accomplished if it's in God's will. If God can resurrect the dead, surely we can ask of Him smaller things

THE COMMAND OR PRAYER USED
Jesus prayed to the Father so that all who heard might believe (v. 41-42). Then He boldly said in a loud voice "Lazarus, come forth." Just three words!

THE LESSON FOR THOSE WHO WATCHED
Jesus was the Messiah!

WHY IT WAS RECORDED IN SCRIPTURE
It shows us that Jesus is greater than death, and that He can literally give new life.

APPLICATION
I will spend time daily in prayer for 5 of my friends that are dead spiritually and ask Jesus to give them life.

MIRACLE	REALM	OCCASION
Lazarus raised (John 11:1-44)	Physical death	He was dead, and four days dead at that
The demon possessed man (Mark 5:1-20)	Spirit world	Slavery (to demon and sins)
The woman with the flow of blood (Luke 8:43-48)	Physical health	desperate (the doctors couldn't help her)

PEOPLE	MEANS	RESULTS	REACTIONS
Lazarus - the dead guy, his sisters, Jesus, and the crowd of mourners	Spoken word "Lazarus come forth"	Lazarus was brought back to life and walked out of the tomb.	Many people believed.
Demon possessed man, Jesus, disciples, local businessmen	Spoken word	He was freed from Legion and "clothed and in his right mind."	Faith in Jesus from the freed man. Anger from the city.
Woman with the flow, Jesus, the crowd, disciples, and Jairus	Touch of His robe	An instant healing	the woman's faith, the disciples confusion, and Jairus worries about the delay - or his faith is built up!

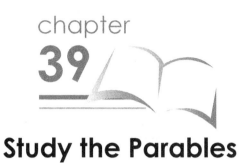

chapter

39

Study the Parables

A parable is a story that uses a natural situation to illustrate and teach a spiritual truth. The word that is translated "parable" in the English Bible literally means, "a comparison of one thing with another." A parable may be a true story, but it doesn't have to be true; the essential element is the spiritual lesson that is being conveyed through the analogy. About thirty-five percent of everything Jesus taught was in the form of parables. Mark 4:11 reveals that He did this in order to hide the truth from the crowds of curiosity seekers that were always following Him, while at the same time teaching spiritual lessons to those who sincerely desired to know. Spiritual guidance is needed, in order to come to a correct interpretation of a parable's meaning. This study method will help you to understand parables while minimizing the chance of misinterpreting them.

The following steps will help you get started *Studying the Parables*:

Step 1 Choose a parable of Jesus' to study
As you read, keep in mind that parables have three main elements: the setting, the story, and the application.

Step 2 Review the three guidelines for correct interpretation
1. <u>Always interpret the story in light of the social customs of the day</u>. Being mindful of the cultural background will help you know how much of the parable is being explained in the passage and how

much of it would have simply been understood in its context, at that time.

2. <u>Never use a parable to establish doctrine</u>. Be wary of any interpretation that does not fall within the clear teaching of Scripture. Parables were meant to be illustrations of biblical truth, not the basis for building new doctrine.

3. <u>Be careful not to take a parable's analogy too far</u>. Do not try to make every point in the parable mean something profound. By doing this, you are in danger of reading more into the analogy than what was originally intended.

Step 3 Write the parable's obvious (natural) meaning

The spiritual lesson is based on the plain meaning of the story. Write down the parable's main points (the people, places, actions, etc.) and your thoughts on its basic meaning.

Step 4 Answer questions to help you interpret the meaning

1. What <u>background information</u> do you know about the common customs and practices of the day?

2. To <u>whom</u> was the parable told? What lesson did they need?

3. Can you <u>put yourself</u> in their place and imagine what they would have thought when they heard the parable? Remember, it was the first time it was ever told.

4. Is the parable <u>interpreted</u> as a whole or in part anywhere else in Scripture? If so, note the Scripture reference and the interpretation.

5. What <u>clues</u> about the parable's interpretation can be found in the immediate context?

Step 5 Write the central spiritual teaching

Remember, a parable is given to set forth, or illustrate, one primary biblical truth. Write down the spiritual lesson that is being taught.

Step 6 Cross-reference this truth

Find any additional Scriptures that reinforce the point being made.

Step 7 Write a modern parable

Rewrite the parable using present-day circumstances to teach the same truth. This is a valuable exercise to see how well you comprehend the parable—writing your own version will necessitate adapting the biblical illustration to a modern setting while retaining the original meaning.

Step 8 Use a commentary to check your interpretation

Once you are done, check your interpretation against commentaries. You should find that your results are similar to what others have found. Chances are, if no one else has interpreted it in the same way you did, you probably need to do a little more work.

Step 9 Apply the truth you learned to your life

Jesus told parables to illustrate a truth that He wanted His followers to observe. Are you living out this truth in your life?

Here is a Partial List of the Parables Told by Jesus

- Drawing in the Net, Matthew 13:47-50
- Laborers in the Vineyard, Matthew 20:1-16
- Lost Money, Luke 15:8-10
- The Faithful Servant, Luke 12:35-48
- The Good Samaritan, Luke 10:30-37
- The Growing Seed, Mark 4:26-29
- The Lost Sheep, Matthew 18:12-14, Luke 15:4-7
- Mustard Seed, Matthew 13:31-32, Mark 4:30-32, Luke 13:18-19
- The Pearl, Matthew 13:45-46
- The Prodigal Son, Luke 15:11-32
- The Sower, Matthew 13:3-23, Mark 4:1-20, Luke 8:5-15
- The Wedding Feast, Matthew 22:1-14, Luke 14:16-24
- Pharisee and the Publican, Luke 18:9-14
- Ten Talents, Matthew 25:14-30, Luke 19:11-27
- Budding Fig Tree, Matthew 24:32-35, Mark 13:28-31
- The Friend at Night, Luke 11:5-8

- The Hidden Treasure, Matthew 13:44
- The Persistent Widow, Luke 18:1-8
- The Leaven, Matthew 13:33, Luke 13:20-21
- The Master and Servant, Luke 17:7-10
- The Rich Fool, Luke 12:16-21
- The Weeds, Matthew 13:24-30
- The Ten Virgins, Matthew 25:1-13
- The Two Debtors, Luke 7:41-47
- The Two Sons, Matthew 21:28-32
- The Unjust Steward, Luke 16:1-9
- Wicked Vinedressers, Matthew 21:33-40, Mark 12:1-9
- The Wise and the Foolish Builders, Matthew 7:24-27
- Unmerciful Servant, Matthew 18:23-35
- Building a Tower and Waging War, Luke 14:28-33
- The Barren Fig Tree, Luke 13:6-9
- The Best Seats, Luke 14:7-14

The next page has a sample of the Study the Parables Bible study method.

STUDY THE PARABLES

TITLE - Parable of the Hidden Treasure

SCRIPTURE - Matthew 13:44

NATURAL MEANING - A man found a great treasure in a field. So, to obtain the treasure, he sold everything he had, and with that money went and bought the field and got the treasure.

BACKGROUND INFO - This process of buying a field seems to be a common practice.

TO WHOM - Jesus was teaching only His disciples (Matthew 13:36).

IF I WERE THERE - I guess it would make sense to believe God's kingdom is something to get really excited about obtaining.

INTERPRETATION IN SCRIPTURE - None

CONTEXT CLUES - The next parable seems very similar (Matthew 13:45).

CENTRAL SCRIPTURAL TEACHING

Here is how I interpret this parable:
- "treasure hidden in a field" = humans
- "which a man" = Jesus (Son of man)
- "found and hid" = Jesus courting His bride
- "and for joy over it" = Jesus loves us
- "goes and sells all that he has" = crucifixion
- "and buys that field" = redemption

So the simple lesson is that Jesus loved us (His "treasure") so much that He gave His life ("all that he has") to purchase us ("buys a field") so that He can have us forever.

CROSS REFERENCE
- John 3:16 - similar to the simple Gospel
- Deuteronomy 7:6 - we are God's treasure
- I Corinthians 6:20 - we were bought with a price
- Hebrews 12:2 - Jesus' joy regarding the cross
- I Peter 1:18-19 - redeemed by Jesus' blood

MODERN PARABLE
"The kingdom of heaven is like a man looking to buy a house, who finds oil in the backyard. He happily sells his car, clothes, and all that he owns to buy this house because he knew it was an overlooked gold mine."

chapter

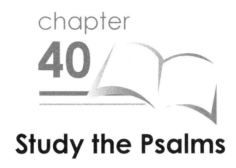

40

Study the Psalms

The book of Psalms gives us some of the most intimate, powerful, and emotionally raw verses in the whole Bible. Throughout the book, we get pictures of the honesty, humility, and holiness by which our relationship with God is to be lived out, every day. Nowhere else in Scripture do we see the inner struggles of the human soul, as it relates to a Holy and awesome God, as clearly as we do in this book. And nowhere else in the Bible do we see an example of such whole-hearted, whole-bodied responsive worship of our Creator. We love the book of Psalms because it puts words of hope and adoration on our lips and sets a standard that we would all like to attain in our relationship with God. It reminds us that God is our Father and not an uncle in a far off land!

The book of Psalms is a book of poetry. Hebrew poetry consists of distinctive elements and since a considerable portion of Scripture is set in this poetic style, it is important to understand those distinguishing features. One helpful hint that is good to remember when it comes to the study of Bible poetry is to read the passage being studied in a modern version. The poetic structure will be more comprehensible when it is read in a contemporary translation.

Follow these steps to begin your *Study of the Psalms*:

Step 1 Categorize by book, subdivision, and subject

The main theme of the Book of Psalms is praise, prayer, and worship to God. In Hebrew, the title of this book means "Praise" or the "Book of Praises." The Book of Psalms has been classified and outlined in a variety of ways. Many view the ancient Hebrew fivefold division (below) as the most helpful. Using this division of the book, choose the category for the Psalm you are studying. Write it on your chart:

1. **Book 1:** Psalms 1-41
   Man, his state of blessedness, fall, and recovery.

2. **Book 2:** Psalms 42-72
   Israel, her ruin, her Redeemer, and her redemption.

3. **Book 3:** Psalms 73-89
   The Sanctuary, looking forward to its establishment in blessing.

4. **Book 4:** Psalms 90-106
   The Earth, blessing needed,anticipated, and enjoyed.

5. **Book 5:** Psalms 107-150
   The Word of God.

Further Subdivisions of the Psalms that You Can Use (if applicable)

- Psalms of Korah, 42-49
- Psalms of Asaph, 73-83
- Golden Psalms, 56-60
- Theocratic Psalms, 95-100
- Hallel Psalms, 113-118
- Psalms of Ascent, 120-134
- Hallelujah Psalms, 146-150
- Messianic Psalms, 22, 23, 40, 50, 68, 96, 98 (and many more!)

Organize the Psalms into These Subject Categories

Prayer, Praise, Petition for Deliverance, Confession of Faith, Confession of Sin, Instruction, Repentance, Intercession, Meditation, Expectation of the Messiah, the Law, History, Doubting, Blessing, and Thanksgiving.

Try coming up with more of your own categories and keep an index to help you group the Psalms in a way that will help you easily revisit them.

Step 2 Old title and new title

Find out what the title means and write it down. Does it set the stage? Now, can you think of your own new title for it? Write down both titles on the top of your paper as a way of remembering the theme.

Step 3 The Psalm's setting

What is the setting and background of the Psalm? Gather whatever information you can on the author, the date, and the one to whom the Psalm was being directed. Use outside helps when necessary.

Step 4 The keys to the Psalm

Read the Psalm and write down the key words (most important words/most repeated words). Then record the key verse: the verse you think is foundational to this psalm.

Step 5 Look for honest emotion towards God

As you read, look for extreme, harsh, or violent language. Does this language confuse you? Such language is acceptable in poetry (not prose) as expressions of the deep emotions of the writer toward God's enemies, not just his own. Are you as honest with God as the psalmist is in his writings?

Step 6 What are the literary features of this poem?

The distinguishing quality of Hebrew poetry is its parallelism—it doesn't rhyme, as we are accustomed to, it blends parallel thoughts together. From the list below see if you can discover the poetic forms. What lines correspond (or parallel) with other lines? Check each for various kinds of parallelism. Using a few sample verses show the literary form's connection; draw arrows between related verses. Do these verses repeat, contrast, expand, or develop the previous thoughts? There are four common parallel forms:

1. <u>Synonymous Parallelism</u>: "Synonymous" means the same. In synonymous parallel Psalms, the second line of the poem repeats the thought of the first line (i.e., Psalm 3:1).

2. <u>Antithetic Parallelism</u>: "Antithetic" means opposite. In antithetic parallelism, the second line is opposite to the first line. However, it is still parallel (or like the first line) because it uses an opposite thought to state a similar truth. This is why it is called antithetic (i.e., Psalm 1:6).

3. <u>Synthetic Parallelism</u>: This type of parallelism is like building with blocks. The second line of the poem adds to or develops the thought of the first line, and all the following lines continue building on the one previous (i.e., Psalm 1:1-2).

4. <u>Emblematic Parallelism</u>: An "emblem" is something that stands for or illustrates something else. For example, the stars in the flag of the United States of America are emblems of the fifty states that are members of the Union. In emblematic parallelism, the second and following lines of a poem are an emblem or illustration of the first line (i.e., Psalm 42:1).

Step 7 The Psalm's relationship to other Scripture

What predictive allusions exist in the Psalm to the New Testament? This should be especially obvious in Messianic Psalms. What allusions to other portions of the Old Testament do you find? Write the verse references.

Step 8 The Psalm's purpose

What is the major lesson being taught throughout the Psalm?

Step 9 Personal application

What doctrinal teachings and practical applications did you find? What spiritual truths are taught here that will help you to live the Christian life? How can you apply the heart of this Psalm?

The next page has a sample of the Study the Psalms Bible study method.

STUDY THE PSALMS

PSALM STUDIED - Psalm 3 (Book 1)

SUBJECT CATEGORY - Petition for Deliverance

OLD TITLE - A Psalm of David when he fled from Absalom his son.

NEW TITLE - Assurance in Adversity

SETTING - The author is David. The story that birthed this psalm of prayer is found in 2 Samuel 15-18 as David's son tried to take the throne. It is directed to those going through persecution in general. This must have crushed David because he loved his son the whole time (2 Samuel 18:5)

KEYWORDS - me (7X), many (2X)
KEY VERSE - v.8 "Salvation belongs to the Lord"

HONEST EMOTION - v.7 "arise!", "save me!" David lets God know he needs help NOW! He is desperate for the Lord to intervene.

"You have broken the teeth of the ungodly" means that God has stopped their mouths from speaking slander in the past and will do so now too.

LITERARY FEATURES
- Synonymous Parallelism - v. 7b

You have struck all my enemies on the cheekbone

You have broken the teeth of the ungodly.

- Contrast - v. 2b-3a

"no help for him... But you... a shield for me"
There is a strong contrast between the
allegation and the psalmist's assurance.

RELATED SCRIPTURE
- Old Testament - 2 Samuel 15:13-17
- New Testament - Romans 8:31

PSALMS PURPOSE - The Lord helps his
people when they are in trouble. It reaffirms
us that we can move from anxiety to
assurance as we pray and trust in God.

PERSONAL APPLICATION - A person I
work with has been attacking me behind
my back with hurtful words. I am going
to let the Lord stop his talk instead of
responding. I will seek peace from God
in prayer each day before work and at
lunch this week.

STUDY METHODS
FOR YOUNGER STUDENTS

*Basic Bible Study Methods Suitable
for Teenage Students*

Each of these methods will help younger students master a basic skill needed to study the Bible. These study methods were designed to help teenagers, and those who teach them, to develop a love and understanding of the Word of God.

chapter

41

Heart Monitor

Have you ever seen an EKG (electrocardiogram) machine at a hospital? This machine monitors the rhythm of a patient's heart and produces a graph with fluctuating lines that charts the internal heart condition. The *Heart Monitor* Bible study method does the same thing, spiritually. It measures our heart excitement over the Scriptures and helps us apply the Great Physicians prescriptions to keep us spiritually healthy. Proverbs 4:23 says "Keep your heart with all diligence, for out of it spring the issues of life." This study method teaches what it means to "keep" our heart.

<u>Skill taught in this method</u>: *Application—Becoming a doer of the Word.*

Follow these simple steps to do a *Heart Monitor* Bible Study:

Step 1 Choose about ten verses that you would like to study

It would be best to choose devotional verses that you have enjoyed in your quiet time recently.

Step 2 Create a heart monitor graph (reference the sample)

Place your verse numbers in the center column on the left side.

Step 3 Place dots on your graph

Read each verse of the passage you are studying. After each verse, put a dot on the graph next to the verse number. The more you are moved by the passage, the closer you should place the dot to the plus side. Be honest. Every verse will not thrill you; but on the other hand, if nothing does, it reveals that there is very little sign of spiritual life.

Step 4 Connect the dots so that you have a graph line

This will show you which verses spiked your internal heart monitor. Now you can quickly look at your graph and see the verses that are speaking to you the loudest.

Step 5 Write your observations for each verse

Reread the passage verse-by-verse and explain why it spoke to your heart. Allow God to speak through your pen as you write the reasons why the Bible is exciting to you. Make note of how the verse encouraged, challenged, or convicted you. You may not have a comment for every verse— that's okay.

Step 6 Write a prescription for your heart

Admitting that you are sick is the first step in coming to the Great Physician. After you see your heart's sinfulness, you know you need some medicine! In this step ask God to show you one specific application that you need to make. If the application is not too personal, share it with someone and ask them to pray that you would take your medicine joyfully.

The next page has a sample of the Heart Monitor Bible study method.

HEART MONITOR

Matthew 7:1-5

1 2 3 4 5

VERSE OBSERVATION

1. This is a bold warning that those who judge will themselves be judged. So don't judge.

2. Here I find that the same standard I use to judge others will be used against me.

3. I'm told that I'm the worst offender, that my sins blind me as I judge others.

4. It's silly to focus on helping other people to sin less when I can stay busy with me!

5. I need to purify my life from sin. This should be my first priority.

PRESCRIPTION

I need to spend some time in prayer asking God to show me my sins. Pointing my finger at myself will be more fruitful.

chapter

42

Funnel It

K nowing how to find the main idea of a passage is key to our under-standing of it. When we can restate the central theme of the Scrip-tures that we are studying in our own words, then we know that we have comprehended the message. Developing good study habits is the first step in training our minds to be able to discern key biblical themes as we read God's Word. Luke 24:45 says, "He opened their understanding, that they might comprehend the Scriptures." If we hope to gain anything of value from our study of the Scriptures, we need to ask God to open our under-standing and help us comprehend what we are reading.

<u>Skill taught in this method</u>: *Identifying the main idea of a passage.*

View the example first and then follow these simple steps to do a *Funnel It* Bible Study:

Step 1 In the funnel's top circle: Write the Scripture out

Writing the passage out will help you to remember it. Educators say that writing something once has the same effect on our retention as reading it eleven times! One of the requirements that God had of Israel's kings was that they were to write "a copy of this law in a book" (Deuteronomy 17:18). The Bible says that Christ has made us kings in His eternal kingdom (Revelation 1:6), so shall we not do the same?

Step 2 In the triangular funnel section: Summarize main ideas

To summarize means to condense a passage down to its essential idea. However, before you can do that you must first fully absorb its meaning. Continue rereading the passage until you can confidently state its central theme briefly and completely.

A summary is shorter than a paraphrase, and generally uses about one word for every four in the original text. When you allow the Word of God to pass through your mind and be reproduced in this way, you will grasp its meaning and significance. When finished, compare your version to the original to be certain that it accurately expresses all the essential information.

Step 3 In the neck of the funnel: Summarize the summary

This is usually one sentence, similar to a newspaper headline. It is one topical sentence, which describes the passage. To help determine the main idea, ask yourself this question: What is being said about the person, thing, or idea?

Step 4 Underneath the funnel flows your personal application

Now that you understand the central idea: What is God saying to your heart personally? All Bible studies should end with application. Unless we are doers of the Word, we are deceiving ourselves.

The next page has a sample of the Funnel It Bible study method.

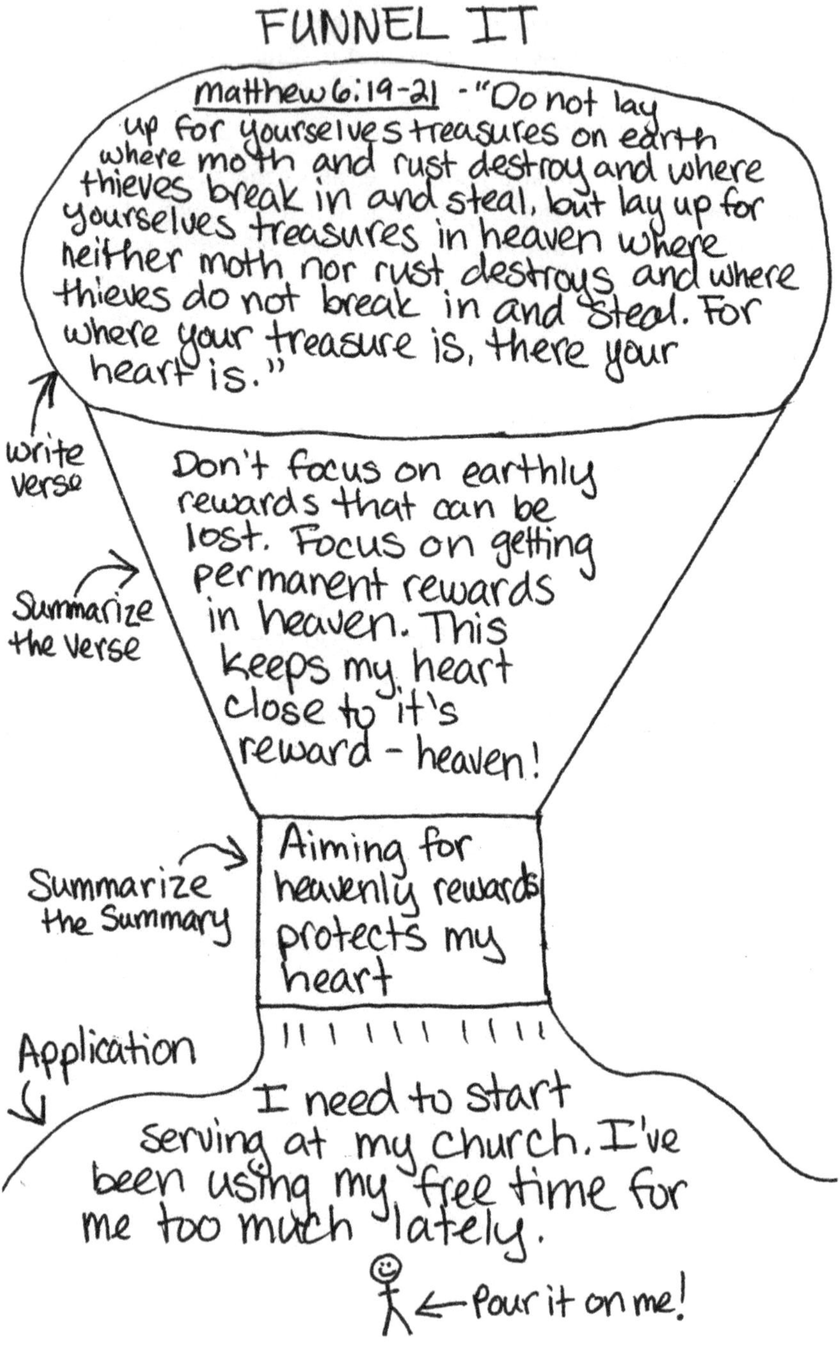

FUNNEL IT

matthew 6:19-21 - "Do not lay up for yourselves treasures on earth where moth and rust destroy and where thieves break in and steal, but lay up for yourselves treasures in heaven where neither moth nor rust destroys and where thieves do not break in and steal. For where your treasure is, there your heart is."

write verse

Summarize the verse

Don't focus on earthly rewards that can be lost. Focus on getting permanent rewards in heaven. This keeps my heart close to it's reward - heaven!

Summarize the Summary

Aiming for heavenly rewards protects my heart

Application

I need to start serving at my church. I've been using my free time for me too much lately.

← Pour it on me!

chapter

43

Weather Report

O ur emotions can be as fickle as the weather. Studying the Bible helps us have victory over our thoughts and emotions, no matter what conditions may be surrounding us. When we know God's Word, we can have the same peace on days when storm clouds roll in as we do on those bright sunny days. The problem is that too often we look at our situation instead of keeping our focus on the God who has control over every circumstance.

<u>Skill taught in this method</u>: *Observation.*

Follow these simple steps to do a *Weather Report* Bible Study:

Step 1 Prayerfully choose a passage to study

Select a small passage for this study, about ten to twenty verses.

Step 2 Draw your blank cloud chart

See the example at the end of this chapter for instructions. You are basically drawing a cloud, lightning bolts, showers, and a rainbow.

Step 3 High pressure

Towards the top of the cloud, write the main idea of the verses that you have read. This should be one sentence that sums up the subject. It should contain not only the topic but what it is saying about the topic.

Step 4 Warning! Storm clouds approaching

Next to the lightning bolt, write any warnings about the danger of not obeying God's specific commands in this passage. If the Holy Spirit has personally warned you about anything, write it in that space too.

Step 5 Showers of blessing

In the Bible, rain is seen as showers of blessings from God. What blessings has He rained down on you as you've studied this passage? If you have learned anything exciting in your time with Him, write it on the chart.

Step 6 A rainbow promise

The first rainbow was recorded in the book of Genesis and signified God's promise to Noah that He would never flood the earth again. What promises does God make in the passage you are studying? Do you have to do anything to obtain those promises? Write your answers next to the rainbow on your chart.

Step 7 Forecast for future applications

Now that you have observed the many parts of this passage it's time to "be a weatherman" and make a forecast. Choose one application that you believe God wants you to make in your life today. What changes, if any, are needed in order to move forward in this direction? Have you been challenged to do something specific for the Lord? Write your answers on the chart.

Now it's time to set deadlines. In reporting the weather, forecasts can range from hourly predictions to extended seven to ten day reports. Ask God to help you set a deadline for completing the application that He has shown you. If you don't forecast it then it will probably never happen.

The next page has a sample of the Weather Report Bible study method.

WEATHER REPORT

Luke 9:23-26

HIGH PRESSURE
"I must take up my cross and follow Jesus"

STORM CLOUD WARNING
If I try to gain the world I will lose my soul.

PROMISE
"IF I lose my life for God, I actually save it!"

Rainbow

SHOWERS OF BLESSING
If I'm not ashamed of God then He won't be ashamed of me!

FORECAST · I need to stop living my life selfishly for me. I need to put my wishes aside to help others get theirs. I'm going to do my sister's chores for one week so she can have more time with her friends.

chapter

44

Climb the Ladder

One of the most useful tools to have when studying Scripture is the ability to see the structure of the paragraph or chapter you are reading. Being able to follow the writer's flow of thought is critical, but it can be difficult to do at times, if you aren't sure how to dissect the text. This Bible study method is going to help you to learn how to outline a passage of Scripture.

<u>Skill taught in this method</u>: *Outlining the text.*

Follow these simple steps to do a *Climb the Ladder* Bible Study:

Step 1 Choose a chapter to study

Step 2 Create a blank ladder chart

See the example at the end of this chapter for instructions on creating this chart. It will look like an actual ladder with a rung for every paragraph division in the chapter.

Step 3 Find the main idea of the whole chapter

Read the chapter twice and then answer these two questions:

1. What is the main topic being discussed in this chapter? For instance, is the main topic love, sin, obedience, temptation, etc.? Your answer to this question should be no more than one or two words.

2. What instruction does this chapter reveal about the main topic? For instance, does it teach you how to love your husband or wife, or warn you that sin leads to death, obedience leads to blessing, temptations can be overcome, etc.

Asking and answering these two questions will help you see the main idea of the chapter. Write this idea at the base of the ladder diagram.

Step 4 Find the main idea of each paragraph

Some Bible translations separate the chapter into obvious paragraph spacing for easy reading. These paragraph divisions in your Bible are a good place to begin dividing the text into sections to create an outline. Ask yourself: What new information, command, exhortation, etc., does this paragraph add to what has already been said about the main topic? On the top rung of the ladder, write your answer to the question as a short paragraph title. Hint: Use a title that will help you relate that idea back to the main topic of the chapter.

Step 5 Find the sub-points of each verse in the paragraph

Each verse contributes to the content and clarity of the paragraph. Under the rung where you placed the paragraph title, summarize the main facts of each verse and write them down in the space provided. Look carefully at each verse, and combine them with others, where appropriate. Use bullet points to organize your thoughts.

Repeat steps 4 and 5 for each paragraph in the chapter.

Note: One problem you may encounter if the chapter is broken into too many paragraphs is that it becomes hard to relate the paragraph to the chapter's main idea. If this occurs, try combining paragraphs.

Step 6 Application

Tracing the flow of a thought in a passage like this can help you come to a better understanding of the biblical principle it teaches. With your new understanding of this passage, can you think of one truth that stands out to you that you feel you need to obey? Whether it is a sin to forsake or a spiritual goal to aim for, make sure you are a doer of the Word.

The next page has a sample of the Climb the Ladder Bible study method.

CLIMB THE LADDER

SCRIPTURE - Philemon

I. Greeting (v.1-3)

   a) From Paul (v.1a)
   b) Written to (v.1-2)
   c) Greetings (v.3)

II. Thanksgiving and Prayer (v.4-7)

   a) Paul's thankfulness (v.4-5)
   b) Paul's prayer (v.6-7)

III. The Plea for Onesimus (v.8-21)

   a) An appeal, not a command (v.8-9)
   b) Paul's plea (v.10-20)
   c) Paul's confidence in Philemon (v.21)

IV. Concluding Remarks (v.22-25)

   a) Request for lodging (v.22)
   b) Greetings from others (v.23-24)
   c) Closing prayer (v.25)

APPLICATION - I think I need to ask God for strength to really forgive Suzy. I will invite her over tonight to set things straight finally. She deserves to be treated like a sister in Christ.

chapter

45

Cross Thoughts

The Bible itself provides the best interpretation of what it means. God repeats ideas many times within a book and throughout the Scriptures in order to unfold the full meaning of what He is saying on every subject and topic. He wants us to get it right. A cross-reference is the easiest way to find related passages of Scripture. It is simply a list of other relevant verses linked together by a common thought, word, topic, or expression. Most Bibles have cross-references in the margins. However, you can also find cross-references in good concordances and study helps like *Naves Topical Bible*. And, as you grow more familiar with God's Word your-self, you will begin to think of your own list of cross-references as you are reading the text. Using cross-references helps us to take all of God's Word into consideration as we study, and provides a better likelihood that we will arrive at a correct interpretation. It takes more time to pause and lookup related Scriptures, but it is a very rewarding and enriching part of your Bible study.

The two types of cross-references that are most helpful are:

1. <u>Words</u>: When the exact same word is used elsewhere.

2. <u>Thoughts</u>: When a similar thought is expressed in another place.

<u>Skill taught in this method</u>: *Cross-Referencing.*

Follow these simple steps to do a *Cross Thoughts* Bible Study:

Step 1 Create a three-column chart
See the example at the end of this chapter for instructions.

Step 2 Choose a paragraph or chapter to study
Read the text in its entirety. Then in column one write the reference number of the first verse you are studying.

Step 3 Find a cross-reference
In the second column, record one or more cross-references for the verse you are studying. At this point, you only need to write down the verse's reference number. Try to find at least one cross-reference for each verse, but you may have up to three.

Usually you will want to follow this order to find your cross-references:

1. Look in the same book of the Bible.
2. Look in other books of the Bible written by the same person.
3. Look in other books of the Bible written at the same time.
4. Look in any other books of the Bible containing a cross-reference.

Step 4 Summarize the cross-reference
Find and read each verse that is listed in your cross-reference. In column three summarize in a brief phrase what the cross-reference says. This will help you to be able to look at your cross-references quickly and remember what they add to your understanding.

Step 5 Review and meditate
Reread the passage. Then spend time reviewing each verse, pausing to read your cross-reference summary phrases. Meditate on how much they add to your understanding of the topic. Often they will even pose new questions that will provoke more research.

Step 6 Application
Prayerfully think about one action step that God is asking you to take based on your new understanding of His truth. Write out your plan.

The next page has a sample of the Cross Thoughts Bible study method.

CROSS THOUGHTS

SCRIPTURE - Psalm 1

VERSE	CROSS REFERENCE	SUMMARY
1	Proverbs 4:14-15	Avoid the evil path
2	Psalm 119:14	Rejoice in God's way
3	Jeremiah 17:8	Be a spiritual tree
4	Job 21:18	The wicked have no roots
5	Matthew 13:49	The angels seperate the bad
6	Psalm 37:18	The righteous inheritance

APPLICATION

To be a spiritual tree that I need to be for my family I need to send my roots down deeper into God's Word. I'm going to make Thursday nights a consistent Bible study time each week.

WRAPPING IT ALL UP

Instruction for Continued Growth
as a Student of the Bible

Some last thoughts on studying the Scriptures and closing advice to help you continue growing as a Bible study student.

chapter

46

Building a Reference Library

Literally hundreds of great books exist that will help you get more out of your Bible study time. It makes sense that you should take advantage of some of these resources. Personally, I believe the following books should be in every Christian's library. If you don't already own them I suggest that they should be the first ten books that you purchase as you start building a study library.

1. Concordance: The best concordances list all the occurrences of every word in the Bible. The concordance at the back of your Bible is helpful at times, but it is limited in size. Therefore, a full concordance is an essential tool for every serious Bible student. One good one is the *Strongest Strong's Exhaustive Concordance.*

2. Bible Dictionary: Bible dictionaries define words found in Scripture with accurate biblical meanings derived from the original languages. Be careful not to rely on regular dictionaries for definitions of biblical words. They may help you understand the English word that was used in the translation, but they will not help you understand the intended original word. One good Bible dictionary is the *New Unger's Dictionary.*

3. Topical Bible: This is similar to a concordance except it lists cross-referenced thoughts instead of exact words. One good topical Bible is the *Naves Topical Bible.*

4. Bible Handbook: This will give you overviews of each book, including background information, archeology, etc. One good handbook is *Halley's Bible Handbook.*

5. <u>Commentaries</u>: Commentaries provide you with a well-studied author's comments on the Scripture you are reading. Hundreds of commentaries are available. One good commentary on the whole Bible is the *Believer's Bible Commentary.*

6. <u>The Treasury of Scripture Knowledge</u>: This is the best cross-reference available. It has more than you'll find in your study Bible. You'll be able to connect the Bible together much better using this tool.

7. <u>Parallel Bible</u>: This will help you quickly compare different translations of the Bible. Many are available; I would recommend one with the New King James Version (NKJV), New Living Translation (NLT), New International Version (NIV), and the Amplified Bible (AMP).

8. <u>Vine's Expository Dictionary</u>: This dictionary helps those who have no background in Hebrew or Greek, to study the meaning of the original biblical words.

9. <u>Manners and Customs in the Bible</u>: This book helps readers gain valuable insight into the cultural background of the biblical world, such as: what people wore, what they ate, what they built, how they mourned, etc.

10. <u>Bible Atlas with Timelines</u>: This gives you maps as they appeared in Bible times compared to today. One good choice is the *Moody Bible Atlas.*

After these ten, I would recommend purchasing some good commentaries.

Websites and Software

There are also many great Bible websites that I would like to tell you about, but in the ever-changing world of the Internet it is better if I list these online so that I can update them consistently. You'll be able to use these sites to lookup verses, read free commentaries, and use a whole library of study resources with the click of a button. While these free websites are very helpful it might be worthwhile to invest in purchasing a software package with more powerful features.

A list of my favorite software packages and links to their websites will be available on this book's website, http://www.LearnToStudyTheBible.com, along with links to buy the ten books listed above.

Some Final Thoughts

I love studying the Scriptures. I love reading and rereading the same stories. I never regret picking up my Bible and spending time with God, learning more about Him and His ways. Wilbur M. Smith said, "There is no sweeter experience than the daily habit of kneeling down at the desk, or table, or chair where we have been studying the Word of God, and pleading the promise we have found before the throne of Grace, or thanking God for some precious truth which our hearts so greatly needed as the Word was opened that morning."

In this book, you have been introduced to many different styles and methods of studying the Scriptures. The absolute best method of studying the Bible is simply to read it, prayerfully, every day, paying close attention to obey what it says. Meditate on the Scriptures and don't stop reading until they have somehow worked their words, message, truth, and revelation of Jesus into the very soul of your being. Nothing extraordinary about that, really, studying the Bible is wonderfully simple. Learn to enjoy God's Word and to apply its truth quickly and you will always find what you seek—His will for your life!

It's been said that the Bible contains the mind of God, the state of man, the way of salvation, the doom of sinners, and the happiness of believers. Its doctrines are holy, its precepts are binding, its histories are true, and its decisions are immutable. Read it to be wise, believe it to be safe, and practice it to be holy. It contains light to direct you, food to support you, and comfort to cheer you. It is the traveler's map, the pilgrim's staff, the pilot's compass, the soldier's sword, and the Christian's charter. It is where we learn that paradise is restored, heaven is opened, and the gates of hell are disclosed. Christ is its grand Subject, our good its design, and the glory of God its end. It should fill the memory, rule the heart, and guide the feet. Read it slowly, frequently, and prayerfully. It is a mine of wealth, a paradise of glory, and a river of pleasure. It is given you in life, will be open at judgment, and be remembered forever. It involves the highest responsibility, rewards the greatest labor, and condemns all who trifle with its holy contents.

Live in The Word

The Word of God is always most precious to the man who relies most upon it. The English preacher, C.H. Spurgeon, recalled a time when God showed Him how to make the Word of God more precious, he wrote "As I sat last year under a wide-spreading beech, admiring that most wonderful of trees, I thought to myself, I do not think half as much of this beech tree as the squirrel does. I see him leap from bough to bough, and I feel sure that he dearly values the old beech tree, because he has his home somewhere inside it in a hollow place, these branches are his shelter, and those beech-nuts are his food. He lives upon the tree. It is his world, his playground, his granary, his home; indeed, it is everything to him, and it is not so to me, for I find my rest and food elsewhere. With God's Word it is well for us to be like squirrels, living in it and living on it. Let us exercise our minds by leaping from bough to bough of it, find our rest and food in it, and make it our all in all. We shall be the people that get the profit out of it if we make it to be our food, our medicine, our treasury, our armory, our rest, our delight. May the Holy Spirit lead us to do this and make the Word thus precious to our souls."

Please Don't Give Up

Undoubtedly, at one time every Christian has resolved, never to let a day go by without spending a portion of it in a focused, prayerful, and enjoyable time alone with God in His Word. However, many have found that after a few short weeks their resolve grows cold. They find their Bibles are going unread days at a time due to a myriad of excuses, such as, they got up too late, or had an unexpected early morning event, or a busy schedule, or even the fact that they have simply become dry or spiritually apathetic. If this is you today, I have one request: Please do not let anything defeat you in this most vital area of Christianity. Knowing God's Word is your secret to victory. Defeat here is defeat all across the board. Make your time with God in His Word the most non-negotiable area of your life and I promise you that you will enjoy the blessings of His presence. The possibilities of Bible study topics and methods are endless; pick one today, and get started. And remember, more important than knowing the Word of God is to know the God of the Word. He is our exceedingly great reward. Bible study is how you get to know God; ignorance of Scripture is ignorance of Christ. So please, cherish your time with God in His Word: Keep His precepts, guard your heart, love His laws, and you will abide in His presence.

> *I rejoice at Your word,*
> *as one who finds great treasure.*
>
> *—Psalm 119:162*

NOTES

Introduction: The Joy of Bible Study

- Skip Heitzig, *Enjoying Bible Study* (Costa Mesa, CA:The Word for Today, 1996) p. 63

- John MacArthur, *How To The Most From God's Word* (Dallas, Texas: Word Publishing, 1997) pp. 153-154

- Harvest International Network, *Creative Bible Study Methods* (Colorado Springs, CO: Harvest International) pp. 103-104

1. Tips for Profitable Bible Study

- W.H. Griffith Thomas, *Methods Of Bible Study* (Chicago, Illinois: Moody Press, 1926) p. 12

2. Observation

- *Precept Austin.* 28 Dec. 2008. Bruce Hurt. <http://preceptaustin.org/observation.htm>.

- Ray E. Baughman, *Personal Bible Study* (Chicago, IL: Moody Press, 1980) p. 61

- Skip Heitzig, *Enjoying Bible Study* (Costa Mesa, CA:The Word for Today, 1996) pp. 61-62

- Josh McDowell, *Guide To Understanding Your Bible* (San Bernardino, CA: Here's Life Publishers, 1982) p. 39; 47

- John MacArthur, *How To The Most From God's Word* (Dallas, Texas: Word Publishing, 1997) pp. 144-145

- Lloyd Perry & Robert Culver, *How to Get More from Your Bible* (Grand Rapids, MI: Baker Book House, 1967) pp. 133-138

3. Interpretation

- *Precept Austin.* 28 Dec. 2008. Bruce Hurt. 22 Apr. 2009 <http://www.preceptaustin.org/the_key_inductive_study_(pt2).htm>.

- Josh McDowell, *Guide To Understanding Your Bible* (San Bernardino, CA: Here's Life Publishers, 1982) p. 69

- John MacArthur, *How To The Most From God's Word* (Dallas, TX: Word Publishing, 1997) p. 163

- Dr. Roy B. Zuck, *Basic Bible Interpretation* (Chicago, Il. David C. Cook: 1991)

- *The Navigators Bible Studies Handbook* (Colorado Springs, CO: NavPress, 1974) p. 17-19; 22

- Skip Heitzig, *Enjoying Bible Study* (Costa Mesa, CA: The Word for Today, 1996) pp. 121-122 and

- Gordon D. Fee & Douglass Stuart, *How to Read the Bible for All Its Worth* (Grand Rapids, MI: Zondervan, 2003) pp. 21-30; 74-74
- Harvest International Network, *Creative Bible Study Methods* (Colorado Springs, CO: Harvest International Institute) p. 69
- Rick Warren, *Rick Warren's Bible Study Methods* (Grand Rapids, MI: Zondervan, 1981) p. 27

4. Application

- Rick Warren, *Rick Warren's Bible Study Methods* (Grand Rapids, MI: Zondervan, 1981) p. 27; 49-60
- *The Navigators Bible Studies Handbook* (Colorado Springs, CO: NavPress, 1974) p. 23
- John MacArthur, Sermon Title *Responding to God's Word* (1 Thessalonians 5:20) GC 52-31
- W.H. Griffith Thomas, *Methods Of Bible Study* (Chicago, Illinois: Moody Press, 1926) p. 112
- *Precept Austin*. 28 Dec. 2008. Bruce Hurt. 22 Apr. 2009 <http://www.preceptaustin.org/the_key_inductive_study_(pt3).htm>.
- Terry Whalin, *Idiot's Guide to Teaching the Bible* (Indianapolis, IN Alpha Group, 2003) p.70
- W. MacDonald & A. Farstad, *Enjoy Your Bible* (Grand Rapids, MI: Gospel Folio Press, 1999) p. 37

5. How to Have Daily Devotions

- Rick Warren, *R. W. Bible Study Methods* (Grand Rapids, MI: Zondervan, 1981) pp. 231-254
- Catherine Martin, *Radical Intimacy, How To Really Have A Quiet Time, A 30 Day Journey* (Palm Desert, California: Quiet Time Ministries Press, 2005) pp. 245-246
- Skip Heitzig, *Enjoying Bible Study* (Costa Mesa, CA: The Word for Today, 1996) p. 35-36
- Wilbur M. Smith, *Profitable Bible Study* (Boston MA: W.A.Wilde Company, 1953) p. 31

6. Daily Bread

- *Help Me With Bible Study*. 22 April. 2009. Douglas Mar. <http://www.helpmewithbiblestudy.org/5Bible/HermChartDevotional.aspx>.
- *Spacepets Bible Study*. 22 April. 2009. Garrett Smith. <http://www.spacepets-bible-study.com/>.

7. Timothy Method

- Kevin Green, *Discipleship Journal's Best Bible Study Methods* (Colorado Springs, Colorado: NAVPRESS, 2002) pp. 33-36

8. SPECS ON
- Ray E. Baughman, *Creative Bible Study Methods* (Chicago, IL: Moody Press, 1976) pp. 64-67

9. Rethink & Restate
10. Alphabet Method

- *The Navigators Bible Studies Handbook* (Colorado Springs, CO: NavPress, 1974) pp. 39-44 and Ray E. Baughman, Personal Bible Study (Chicago, IL: Moody Press, 1980) p. 267

11. One At a Time

- *The Navigators Bible Studies Handbook* (Colorado Springs, CO: NavPress, 1974) pp. 36-38

12. Six-Searches
- Roy B Zuck, *The Speaker's Quote Book* (Grand Rapids, MI: Kregel Publications, 1997) p.39

13. Exhaust Your Question
14. 5 Ps Method

- Ray E. Baughman, *Personal Bible Study* (Chicago, IL: Moody Press, 1980) p. 263-264

15. Verse By Verse Charting

- *Each New Day A Miracle.* 22 April. 2009. Peter Rhebergen. <http://www.eachnewday.com/HowToStudyTheBible/>.
- Wilbur M. Smith, *Profitable Bible Study* (Boston MA: W.A.Wilde Company, 1953) p.37

16. Chapter Overview Method

- Wilbur M. Smith, *Profitable Bible Study* (Boston MA: W.A.Wilde Company, 1953) pp. 28-33
- Lloyd Perry & Robert Culver, *How to Get More from Your Bible* (Grand Rapids, MI: Baker Book House, 1967) pp. 108-109

17. Chapter Details Study
- *Help Me With Bible Study.* 22 April. 2009. Douglas Mar. <http://www. helpmewithbiblestudy.org/5Bible/HermChartChapterAnalysis.aspx>.

18. Book Overview Method
- Ray E. Baughman, *Creative Bible Study Methods* (Chicago, IL: Moody Press, 1976) pp. 88-92

19. Book Details Method

- Skip Heitzig, *Enjoying Bible Study* (Costa Mesa, CA: The Word for Today, 1996) p. 48

- John MacArthur, *How To The Most From God's Word* (Dallas, TX: Word Publishing, 1997) p. 166
- *Help Me With Bible Study*. 22 April. 2009. Douglas Mar. <http://www.helpmewithbiblestudy.org/5Bible/HermChartBookSynthesis.aspx>.

20. Bible Character Study

- Wilbur M. Smith, *Profitable Bible Study* (Boston MA: W.A.Wilde Company, 1953) pp. 44-46
- R.A. Torrey, *How to Study The Bible For Greatest Profit* (Grand Rapids, MI: Baker Book House, 1985) p. 63
- John B. Job, *How To Study The Bible* (Downers Grove, Illinois: Intervarsity Press, 1972) p. 46
- *Help Me With Bible Study*. 22 April. 2009. Douglas Mar. <http://www.helpmewithbiblestudy.org/5Bible/HermChartCharacterQuality.aspx>.

21. Biblical Topics

- Irvin L. Jensen, *Enjoy Your Bible* (Minneapolis, MI: World Wide Publications, 1969) pp. 111-116.

22. Bible Themes

- *Each New Day A Miracle*. 22 April. 2009. Peter Rhebergen. <http://www.eachnewday.com/HowToStudyTheBible/>.

23. Word Studies

- Wilbur M. Smith, *Profitable Bible Study* (Boston MA: W.A.Wilde Company, 1953) p. 41
- *Help Me With Bible Study*. 22 April. 2009. Douglas Mar. <http://www.helpmewithbiblestudy.org/5Bible/HermChartWordStudy.aspx>.

24. Translation Comparison

- Ray E. Baughman, *Creative Bible Study Methods* (Chicago, IL: Moody Press, 1976) pp. 43-50

25. Messy Bible

- Sue Kline, *Discipleship Journal's Best Bible Study Methods: Making Your Mark* (Colorado Springs, CO:Nav Press, 2002) pp. 53-56

26. Modern Issues

- John B. Job, *How To Study The Bible* (Downers Grove, Illinois: Intervarsity Press, 1972) p. 86

27. Thirty Days Each

- John MacArthur, *How To The Most From God's Word* (Dallas, Texas: Word Publishing, 1997) pp. 157-160

28. Vantage Point

- Katrina Baker, *Discipleship Journal's Best Bible Study Methods: Thickening the Plot* (Colorado Springs, CO:Nav Press, 2002) pp. 73-76

29. Skeptics Method

- Barry, John D, *Bible Study Magazine: Bible Study Anyhwhere*, Mar-Apr 2009, pg. 14.

30. Royal Wisdom

- Nativity Abrecia, *Discipleship Journal's Best Bible Study Methods: The Treasures of Kings* (Colorado Springs, CO:Nav Press, 2002) pp. 65-66

31. Categorizing Proverbs
32. Meeting Jesus

- Cindy Hyle Bezek, *Discipleship Journal's Best Bible Study Methods* (Colorado Springs, CO: NAVPRESS, 2002) pp. 89-92

33. Twenty Jesus Questions

- Todd D. Catteau, *Discipleship Journal's Best Bible Study Methods* (Colorado Springs, Colorado: NAVPRESS, 2002) pp. 93-96

34. The Commands Of Jesus

- Peter Theodore, *Discipleship Journal's Best Bible Study Methods* (Colorado Springs, CO: NAVPRESS, 2002) pp. 97-99

35. Truly, Truly

- Todd D Catteau, *Discipleship Journal's Best Bible Study Methods* (Colorado Springs, CO: NAVPRESS, 2002) pp. 101-102

36. Study The Types Of The Bible

- R.A. Torrey, *How to Study The Bible For Greatest Profit* (Grand Rapids, MI: Baker Book House, 1985) p. 65-67
- Harvest International Network, *Creative Bible Study Methods* (Colorado Springs, CO: Harvest International Institute) p.220
- William MacDonald & Arthur Farstad, *Enjoy Your Bible* (Grand Rapids, Michigan: Gospel Folio Press, 1999) pp. 41-43

37. Study The Prayers Of The Bible

- Lloyd Perry & Robert Culver, *How to Get More from Your Bible* (Grand Rapids, MI: Baker Book House, 1967) pp.151-156
- Wilbur M. Smith, *Profitable Bible Study* (Boston MA: W.A.Wilde Company, 1953) pp. 48-50

38. Study The Miracles Of The Bible

- Lloyd Perry & Robert Culver, *How to Get More from Your Bible* (Grand Rapids, MI: Baker Book House, 1967) pp. 157-163

39. Study The Parables Of The Bible

- Lloyd Perry & Robert Culver, *How to Get More from Your Bible* (Grand Rapids, MI: Baker Book House, 1967) pp. 164-170

40. **Study The Psalms Of The Bible**
- Lloyd Perry & Robert Culver, *How to Get More from Your Bible* (Grand Rapids, MI: Baker Book House, 1967) pp. 169-180

41. Heart Monitor
- Ray E. Baughman, *Creative Bible Study Methods* (Chicago, IL: Moody Press, 1976) pp. 13-20

42. Funnel It
- Ray E. Baughman, *Creative Bible Study Methods* (Chicago, IL: Moody Press, 1976) pp. 30-35

43. Weather Report
- Ray E. Baughman, *Creative Bible Study Methods* (Chicago, IL: Moody Press, 1976) pp. 54-58

44. Climb The Ladder
- Ray E. Baughman, *Creative Bible Study Methods* (Chicago, IL: Moody Press, 1976) pp. 59-64

45. Cross Thoughts
- Ray E. Baughman, *Creative Bible Study Methods* (Chicago, IL: Moody Press, 1976) pp. 50-54

46. Building A Reference Library

47. Some Final Thoughts
- Wilbur M. Smith, *Profitable Bible Study* (Boston MA: W.A.Wilde Company, 1953) p. 69

---

http://www.LearnToStudyTheBible.com

Visit the book's website and use the password *Psalm119:162,* for complete access to all of the exclusive bonus resources that purchasing this book entitles you to. If you've enjoyed using any of the methods in this book please submit your completed studies (scanned or typed) so that we can post them on the website for others to view. The online store has additional Bible study resour created by Pastor Andy to aid your Bible study time. If you time, please visit the website and post a book review.

Pastor Andy Deane is available to teach a Bible study at your church, youth group, or Christian school. Plea website for sample seminar topics and contact inform

CPSIA information can be obtained
at www.ICGtesting.com
Printed in the USA
BVHW070927201219
567321BV00001B/89/P